Hamlyn Colour Guides

Ornamental Birds

Hamlyn Colour Guides

Ornamental Birds

by Stanislav Chvapil

Illustrated by
Libuše and Jaromír Knotek

HAMLYN

Translated by Dana Hábová
Graphic design by Jaromír Knotek
Designed and produced by Artia for
Hamlyn Publishing,
a division of The Hamlyn Publishing Group Limited,
Bridge House, London Road,
Twickenham, Middlesex, England

Second impression 1986

ISBN 0 600 35647 7
Printed in Czechoslovakia
3/15/08/51–02

CONTENTS

Advice for beginners 6
Cages and aviaries 6
Buying and transporting birds 11
Quarantine and acclimatization 12
Food and feeding 13
Colour illustrations 15

Characteristics of bird groups 208
Galliformes (Game birds) 208
Columbiformes (Pigeons and doves) 210
Trochiliformes (Hummingbirds) 211
Piciformes (Woodpeckers and allies) 212
Psittaciformes (Parrots) 213
Passeriformes (Songbirds) 214

Hygiene and veterinary problems in bird-keeping 215
Parasitic diseases 216
Contagious diseases 217
Diseases of the digestive tract 218
Respiratory diseases 219
Eye inflammations 219
Disorders of the metabolism 219
Egg binding 220
Overgrown claws and beaks 220
Index 221

ADVICE FOR BEGINNERS

Anyone wishing to keep ornamental and aviary birds should first consider what conditions the birds can be offered. A town dweller without a garden should choose bird species which can be kept in a room, on a balcony or on a terrace. A different type of bird is suitable for owners who can transfer their pets to an outdoor summer aviary. There is also a difference between an aviculturist who intends to breed birds, and a person who merely wishes to keep a single talking pet for entertainment. Initially, undemanding species should be tried, and only after acquiring sufficient knowledge and experience, should rare and more delicate birds be bought. Some hardy species include Canaries, Bengalese Finches, Zebra Finches, some species of pheasant, Java Sparrows, weavers, Budgerigars and Red-rumped Parrots. Cages, aviaries and the other necessary equipment should not be purchased until the choice of birds has been made, as different species of birds have different requirements.

CAGES AND AVIARIES

A cage is usually advisable for a single pair or a small number of birds to be kept indoors. A suitable type is a box (Fig. 1) with the front wall made of wire netting. Cages used for nesting can have doors on the sides to which nestboxes, Canary-type boxes, and so on may be affixed. Round cages with turrets and other ornaments are unsuitable. The interior equipment depends on the species to be kept.

One of the basic principles of bird-keeping is the bigger the cage, the better it is for the birds' health. It should measure at least 100 by 40 by 70 centimetres. In cages for songbirds of the family Estrildidae, the wires should be 10 to 12 centimetres apart. In cages for larger species, the spacing should prevent the birds from sticking their heads out. Some aviculturists recommend horizontal wires instead of the traditional vertical ones; the birds can be observed better and they do not wear out their tail feathers so much. Larger cages are usually covered with wire netting. Both wires and netting should be painted with a non-poisonous black paint.

Apple-tree, willow and birch branches and twigs of different size and thickness may be placed in the cage, or perches made of hazelnut, ash or elder twigs. The cage must never be so crowded with branches that the birds can only hop and not fly around. The branches must be placed with care since if they are situated too close to a wall, the birds can wear out or break their tail feathers. The perches must never be

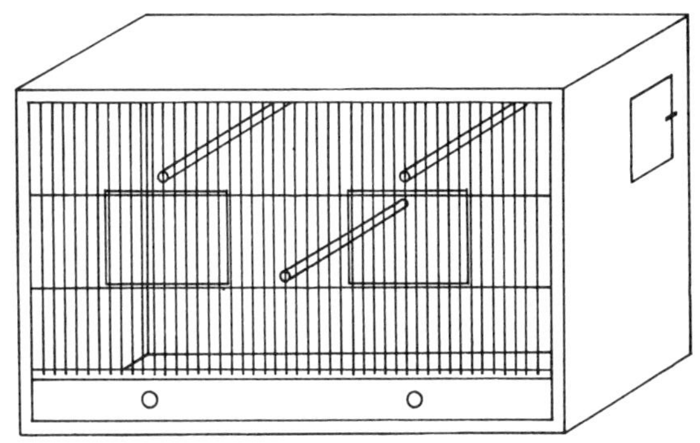

Fig. 1. Box-type cage with an all-wire front wall and one or two doors. Doors can also be situated at the sides. The double, pull-out bottom facilitates cleaning.

so thin that the birds can span them with their toes. A clump of reed stems or coniferous twigs should be put into a cage where small songbirds are meant to breed, as the birds build a nest in the vegetation. The bottom should be covered with clean river sand, or, in case of birds having thin excrements, with peat or paper which are daily replaced. A protective band of glass prevents excrements, seed husks and other food remnants from falling out of the cage. A tray containing water for bathing is hung outside a small cage or placed on the bottom of a roomier one.

It is important to keep the cage in a permanent place; the birds soon get used to it, and they are adversely affected by any change.

A cage with the front wall or all walls made of glass is a vitrine. The larger it is, the better. To improve air circulation, only the lower halves of the lateral walls can be of glass, the upper parts and the ceiling being of wire netting or organdy. The glass walls must be easily removable for regular cleaning. Thoughtful placing of feeding and drinking vessels and perches prevents frequent and heavy soiling of the glass. The framework should be wooden, preferably of a colour matching the furniture in the room. A light-coloured, non-poisonous paint must be used on the inside walls, especially on the solid rear wall. Bulbs, fluorescent or infra-red lamps, shielded by plexiglass, are used to light the vitrines. The interior is planted with resistant, non-poisonous evergreen vegetation, such as moss, producing a highly decorative look. The birds, however, soon destroy the greenery, and new plants have to be added. Consequently, although the glass vitrines are very attractive and impressive, they are not suitable for consistent breeding of small songbirds.

A stand is suitable for large and reliably tame parrots. It is either a strong branch or a miniature tree used for climbing. The size and height are optional. The stand is fitted to a wooden, metal-covered

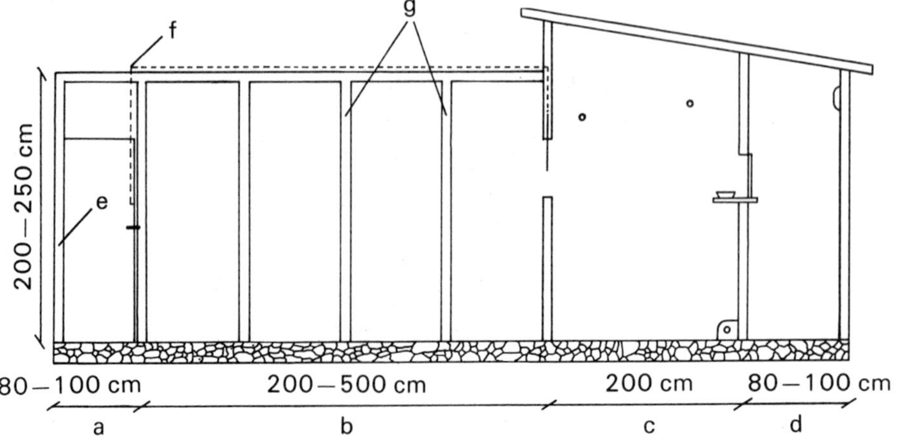

Fig. 2. Lateral view of an outdoor aviary for larger species of parrot: a — protective corridor, b — outside space for flying, c — inside sheltered space, d — manipulating corridor, e — height of aviary, f — controlling line, g — metallic or wooden framework.

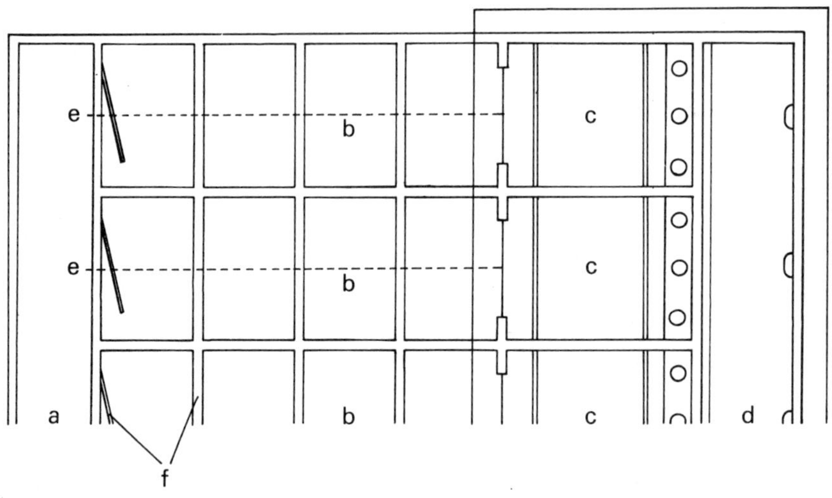

Fig. 3. Top view of a series of outdoor aviaries for larger species of parrot: a — protective corridor, b — outside space for flying, c — inside sheltered space, d — manipulating corridor, e — controlling lines, f — framework

tray filled with sand, in which the excrements and food remnants are gathered. Solid porcelain vessels with food and drinking water are affixed to the stand. This device is suitable mainly for tame macaws, amazons, cockatoos and large species of lory. The parrots may sometimes take a long time to get used to the stand. They are transferred to a cage for the night. Parrots are sometimes chained to a stand, which is harmful, injurious and unsightly. Metallic stands which cannot be destroyed even by birds with very powerful beaks are available in pet shops.

An outdoor aviary is an ideal place to keep a bird in. Before building it, however, the aviculturist should decide which bird species will be kept there. Aviaries differ in size and detail. They can be built several in a row or individually, depending on the landscape of the garden and the aviculturist's taste. An aviary should have two main sections: outside space for flying and inside sheltered space or at least a small shelter. The depth should surpass the width. Aviary dimensions for large parrots are stated in Fig. 2. The foundations, preferably made of concrete, should be at least 50 centimetres deep. The height of 200 to 250 centimetres is sufficient for most birds, except pheasants. The external framework is wooden or composed of metallic tubes. It is covered with wire netting, the mesh size being chosen according to the species. The durability of the wire netting depends on the gauge; it must be given a coating of protective paint such as bitumen varnish. Bricks, wood, transite, and so on, are used to build the inside sheltered part; the building material must be strong enough to prevent mice from getting in. The space for flying is separated from the interior by a double-glass partition or a partition made of glass bricks, to let light in. The entry, which is situated in the upper third of the partition, should be just big enough to let the birds fly in safely. The entry is closed by a strong metal sheet fitted to a thick line stretched over a pulley above the flying space to the front wall. Good roof insulation is a must in the inside shelter to prevent overheating in summer. Polystyrene and glass wool are suitable for insulation.

If several aviaries are built in a row, a feeding and manipulating corridor (Fig. 3) should be constructed behind the inside section. Heating can also be installed in this corridor, and the heat distributed through pipes along the base of the inside section. Sufficient lighting is necessary in the feeding corridor and in the interior, particularly in winter when daylight has to be artificially extended. The artificial light is used in the morning, and an electric time switch is recommended, set, for example, at 4 a.m.

For most of the year, food is passed into the interior through an opening in the corridor. There is also a door and an observation window in the wall. A protective corridor can be built in front of the outside flying space, to hinder direct frontal winds and stop predators, mainly cats. This corridor is also used to watch the birds or to feed them in the summer months. A wall, some 40 to 100 centimetres high, is raised around an aviary with pheasants or other fowl-like birds, to protect them from wind and disturbance.

The inside equipment is chosen according to the species of birds housed. It should comprise only the vital aids — feeding vessels, trays with drinking water, and so on. The birds need as much space as possible for flying, and planting of greenery should be carefully planned. Parrots do not need live greenery, while a pheasant aviary can be planted with shrubs or trees which are regularly trimmed. If keeping pheasants, one does not have to separate the two parts of the aviary. Plants suitable for aviaries include box tree (*Buxus*), arbor vitae (*Thuja*), juniper (*Juniperus*), spruce (*Picea*), hornbeam (*Carpinus*), beech (*Fagus*), oak (*Quercus*). Songbirds also appreciate the snowberry (*Symphoricarpos*), currant (*Ribes*), elder (*Sambucus*), willow (*Salix*), privet (*Ligustrum*), and climbing plants such as hops (*Humulus*), knotgrass (*Polygonum*), *Calystegia* and others. The bottom of the aviary, covered with soil, is sown with grass. Songbirds welcome concrete pools, sprinklers or self-cleaning miniature pools with running water to wash away dirt. To produce a pleasant visual impression, the surroundings of the aviary are planted. The corners can be covered with climbing plants, such as clematis, or with tall tufts of ornamental grasses. Roses (*Rosa*), sage (*Salvia*) or begonias (*Begonia*) look well in front of the aviary.

An outdoor aviary can also be erected on a balcony or terrace, preferably on the southern side of the building, although the western and eastern sides are also satisfactory. The aviary has to be sheltered from wind and rain on the sides and on top, as with garden aviaries. The entry door has to be secured to prevent the birds from escaping; a small antechamber is a useful security measure.

An indoor aviary can be installed in a room or attic. A carefully maintained aviary can be an attractive feature of an interior design. Its size depends on the available space; the floor can be the bottom of the aviary, and the ceiling can be its roof. The framework is made either of iron or wood and covered with wire netting. The foundation is about 20 centimetres high and the bottom must not have any cracks. The front wall can be made of glass, while the rear one and one of the lateral walls can be formed by the walls of the room. The entry is usually situated on the side. The interior must have sufficient daylight or artificial light. Live shrubs in large flowerpots can be put in an aviary where a small number of songbirds is kept. A large branch, preferably pine, may be fitted to one side of the aviary, and another branch affixed to the opposite wall together with a clump of reed stems, where the birds usually build their nest.

Birds' rooms are rooms with aviary equipment, where the birds can move about freely. The rooms are heated and the birds are protected from rain, fog, and so on. The windows should be as large as possible, facing east or south, to let sufficient sunshine in. Frames with thick wire netting are placed in front of the windows to that they can be left open in summer to aerate the room. A spacious all-wire cage can be installed in front of the window in the summer months, allowing the birds to bask in the sun or bathe in the rain. The walls of the room are painted white or whitewashed. For hygienic reasons, the painting is done every year and disinfectant is added to the paint. In autumn and winter, natural daylight is extended by artificial light. The light and heat sources should be covered with wire netting.

The equipment is the same as for an outdoor or indoor aviary, adapted to the species to be kept in the birds' room. A part of the floor, which should be impermeable, is covered with clear river sand, and the other part is covered with peat or sawdust. If the birds' room is situated behind a door through which the birds could fly out, a simple antechamber made of wire-netting over a frame can be put in front of it.

BUYING AND TRANSPORTING BIRDS

When the cage or aviary is ready, one can proceed to buy the birds. Beginners should try out some common and cheap species to acquire sufficient skill. If possible, the birds should be selected personally in specialized shops or purchased from breeders. For breeding purposes, a pair or more should be acquired. It is advisable to get young birds and to rear them into adulthood. It is usually preferable to obtain several unrelated specimens of the same species and allow the birds to choose their own partners. Before buying the birds, their external appearance and behaviour should be observed carefully. Smooth and rich plumage, clear eyes and lively movement signal good health. The bird's requirements, way of feeding and diet, characteristic behaviour, and so on, should be investigated.

Wooden transport boxes (Fig. 4) are best suited for transferring birds from one place to another. They are available in specialized shops or can be made from thin planks or plywood 1.5 to 2 centimetres thick, the size of the box depending on the size of the bird. A grate or wire netting is inserted in one of the walls, the wire gauge being adjusted to the species of bird. Some transport boxes have a solid wall with airing holes in front of the grate. The door must be well secured, for example, with a screw. The birds are put inside by hand and transported singly or in groups, according to species and

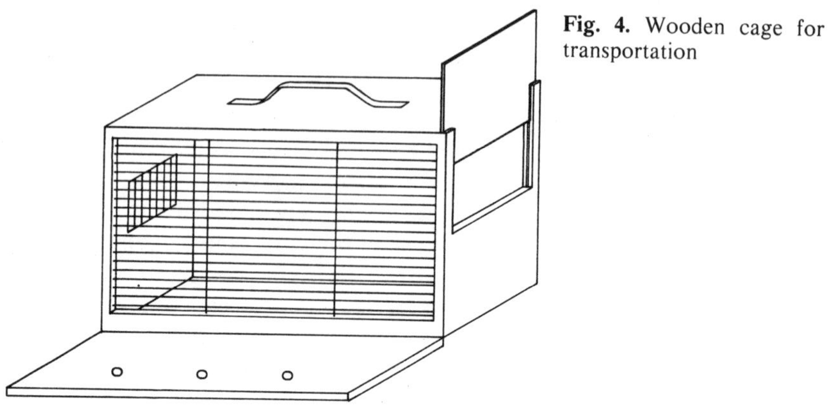

Fig. 4. Wooden cage for transportation

mutual tolerance. Transport boxes with several compartments can also be built.

Newly acquired birds should be situated in a special cage and kept under observation for a few days before being released. They must not be taken out by hand, but left to fly out into their new residence. The birds should at first be served the food they are used to.

QUARANTINE AND ACCLIMATIZATION

If birds are brought from abroad or purchased from an import company, they should be put in quarantine, which serves to prevent contagious and parasitic diseases from developing among the established birds. The duration of quarantine is determined by veterinary rules according to the species of bird.

The birds should be housed in a room completely separated from the premises where the other birds live. The temperature for tropical birds must be kept at 20 to 25 degrees Centigrade. Newspapers or blotting papers on the bottom of the quarantine cage are replaced daily by fresh ones. The newly imported birds have to undergo gradual acclimatization, that is, to adapt themselves to new living conditions. They progressively adjust to the diet which is the most suitable in captivity, and they are served camomile infusion or tea, which is gradually diluted until pure water is served. The temperature is also reduced by stages. The new birds must be handled after the established ones so that any infection will not be spread among the healthy individuals. Strict personal hygiene must be observed. Most well-acclimatized birds become resistant and can withstand sudden changes in their living conditions.

FOOD AND FEEDING

Food for birds is a source of energy, and must also contain the substances necessary for body construction and for proper functioning of their organs. Variety and quality of food is a must; a properly balanced diet results in good health and affects many other factors.

Every meal has to offer variety. An aviculturist will learn by experiment what his charges like to eat. It is important to let the birds choose from a broad range of foodstuffs. The food has to be fresh, clean and without additives, and green food should be thoroughly washed. It is difficult to establish the feeding dosage per bird, since food consumption varies with the species and according to season. Food requirements increase particularly in the breeding season.

Food is divided into five basic groups:

1) Plant food is the main source of glycines, vegetable proteins, vitamins, minerals and water. It is the basic diet for most pigeons and doves, game birds, parrots and songbirds. The bulk of this diet is formed by seeds and grains. These differ in nitrogen content, have a low fat level, and their fibres facilitate digestion. Minerals contained in seeds include phosphorus. Vitamins to be found comprise the vitamin B family, sometimes vitamins A and D, and germinating grains are rich in vitamin E.

Green food is a vital dietary component, needed by almost all species of birds. Its value consists mainly in the content of iodine, sodium chloride, manganese and vitamins. Birds also need fruit and vegetables. Most species should be given apples and pears throughout the year, and fruit such as apricots, peaches, plums, gooseberries, currants, grapes and strawberries seasonally. Some parrots, pigeons and doves are given bananas, oranges, figs and other tropical fruits. The fruit should be served in small quantities and the excrements checked, because fruit-eating birds are susceptible to diarrhoea. Carrots are an important item in a bird's diet due to their high contents of carotene and sugars and other favourable dietetic effects. Carrots are suitable for almost all species of birds and may be served whole or grated and added to mixtures. Fresh twigs and branches of fruit trees, willow and maple are given to parrots to nibble on. From these the birds obtain cellulose, vital trace elements and vitamins.

2) Animal food is the principal source of animal proteins which birds need, particularly when the young are forming. It cannot be replaced by any other material, and is vital during the breeding period. In addition to insects or their various developmental stages such as larvae, Enchytraeids (*Enchytraeus albidus*) and water fleas (Cladocera), the animal diet includes milk, eggs and honey. A valuable source of

proteins, milk, must be odourless, never sour, and boiled before it is served. Eggs of domestic hens comprise 12 per cent proteins, about 12 per cent fatty substances, 15 per cent minerals and 7 per cent water. They also contain vitamins. Some birds drink raw eggs, but hard-boiled eggs are more advisable. Egg mixture (soft food) is made from grated hard-boiled eggs, breadcrumbs and grated carrots; grated chickweed, nettles, dandelion leaves and so on, can also be added. If this mixture is supplemented with ant cocoons, dried mayflies (Ephemeroptera) or mealworm larvae cut to pieces, it becomes the so-called Nightingale mixture. The Thrush mixture is obtained by adding grated curds, minced boiled or raw meat and berries. Honey is an antibiotic and contains 75 per cent sugar. It is served diluted in the proportion of a tablespoon of honey to 1 litre of water.

3) Vitamins and minerals are neither building substances nor energy sources, but they are indispensable for survival. Birds which have a varied and rich diet, and live in a sunny environment, receive all the vitamins they need and do not suffer from avitaminosis. Deficiencies occur mainly in vitamins A, B, D and E. Vitamin A enhances a bird's resistance to infection. Good sources are carrots, fresh vegetables, nettles, egg yolk and cod-liver oil. Vitamin B comprises a complex of vitamins which are necessary for nervous activity and the usage of glycides, fats and vegetable proteins. It is contained in dried yeast which is added to soft food. Vitamin D is important for the absorption of calcium and phosphorus in the bird's organism. It is produced in the body in the presence of sunlight. In winter, it is given to the birds in cod-liver oil (1 teaspoon per 1 kilogram of grains). Vitamin E, which promotes fertility and positively affects the nervous system, is present in germinating grains or in wheat-germ oil; a few drops are added to egg mixtures. Synthetic vitamin pills, soluble in water, are supplied about once a week during the winter months. Insoluble multivitamin concentrates (Multibionta or Protovit) are served in soft food.

Birds receive minerals in food and rarely suffer deficiencies. A regular supply of minerals is necessary before and during the breeding season and in the moulting period. Sources of minerals include crushed egg shells, cuttlefish bones, old plaster and cooking salt. Specialized shops offer so-called grit stones and mineral stones.

4) Supplements necessary for good digestion include sand, charcoal and decaying wood. Sand helps to pulverize food in the stomach, while charcoal absorbs redundant gases and liquids in the intestines and contains traces of calcium, phosphorus and potash.

5) Water is indispensable for all biological processes. It must be unpolluted, potable, always fresh and served in sufficient quantity. It should be changed once to several times a day.

COLOUR ILLUSTRATIONS

King Quail
Coturnix chinensis

Phasianidae

Its diminutive size (13—14 centimetres) makes the King Quail a highly popular cage and aviary bird. If possible it should be kept in a garden aviary sown with a mixture of grass seeds during the summer. Quails can be kept with various small gallinaceous birds and other species. The King Quail is monogamous and should therefore be kept in pairs. The hen builds a nest in the thickest plant cover, weaving a few stalks above the nesting cup into a roof. She lays four to six olive-brown eggs with dark brown or black spots, which are incubated by both parents for 16 days. The newly hatched striped chicks are the size of a bumblebee, and develop quickly. Their wing and tail feathers start growing at 2 to 3 days of age, and they undertake their first flights after 14 days. They are fully fledged when they are 6 weeks old.

The female can breed in a cage, but the eggs have to be transferred to an incubator, and the hatched chicks are kept in a heated box. The young are fed fresh ant cocoons, chopped mealworm larvae, grated hard-boiled eggs, poppyseed and finely chopped green food. Mineral supplements must be given. The basic diet of adult King Quails is small varieties of millet, canary seed, poppyseed, and occasional insects. Green food is essential, particularly for cage birds. Fine sand should be provided for the birds to wallow in.

The handsomely coloured male (1) differs markedly from the brownish hen (2). Breeders have created a silver-coloured mutation, in which the difference between the male (3) and female (4) is less pronounced than in the wild form.

In the wild, the King Quail is distributed in ten subspecies from India and Sri Lanka to south-eastern China and Taiwan, the Indonesian Archipelago, New Guinea, New Caledonia, the Bismarck Archipelago and the coastal areas of northern, eastern and south-eastern Australia. It frequents marshland and grassy steppes. In cultivated areas, the King Quail visits rice paddies after the harvest. The King Quail is a reluctant flier, preferring to run when danger threatens.

4 ♀
3 ♂
1 ♂
2 ♀

Californian Quail
Lophortyx californica

Phasianidae

This beautiful miniature fowl is best displayed in an indoor or garden aviary. It reaches a length of 24 to 25 centimetres, 8 centimetres of which is the tail. During the day, the quails forage on the ground or wallow in fine sand. They roost in branches at night. Adult birds are fed on millet, oats, barley, berries, occasional ant cocoons and meal-worm larvae.

The hen lays a large clutch of creamy white eggs with dark brown spots in a shallow depression in the ground. When thirty eggs are laid, it is recommended to separate the pair. Since the female rarely incubates her own eggs, these should be given to a dwarfish domestic hen or duck which will rear the young. The eggs can also be placed into an incubator and the chicks into a box fitted with an electric bulb. The young hatch in 22 days. They are fed ant cocoons, chopped meal-worm larvae, egg mixture, protein mixture for chickens, chopped nettles, milfoil, dandelion, and so on. Nine-day-old chicks can fly up on a branch. The chicks are independent after 4 weeks, and they can then be given small grains. The quails can be left throughout the winter in an outdoor aviary provided with a shelter. Other small aviary birds should not be kept with the quails, because at night they would be disturbed by the roosting fowls.

2 ♀

The natural habitat of the Californian Quail is mixed and deciduous woods covering the slopes and valleys stretching from south-western Oregon to the Californian Peninsula. The birds are rather timid and cautious. The male (1) has a crest of four dark feathers, while the female (2) lacks this ornament. Outside the nesting period the populations live in flocks which break up into pairs in early April. The male stands guard near the brooding female. If the hen perishes or falls prey to a carnivore, the male takes over the incubation of the eggs (3) and rears the offspring. The chicks are otherwise looked after by the hen while the cock stays nearby.

The first Californian Quails were brought to Europe from the Pacific coast of North America in 1837. They have been successfully introduced into the states of Washington, Utah, Arizona, New Mexico, and into Hawaii, New Zealand and Chile.

1 ♂

Reeve's Pheasant
Syrmaticus reevesii

Phasianidae

This majestic pheasant can be kept in a large aviary or, preferably, loose in a garden, although the birds have to be well tamed for the latter. This is achieved by constant contact with the chicks, including feeding them from the hand. The cock reaches a length of over 200 centimetres, more than three-quarters of which is the tail. This is composed of twenty tail feathers, both central pairs measuring as much as 150 to 180 centimetres. The hen measures 75 centimetres, out of which some 40 centimetres are taken up by the tail.

The rear part of the garden should be planted with dense bushes in which the three or four hens per male can hide. The hen lays eight to fifteen greenish-brown eggs in a simple nest lined with leaves, and incubates them for 24 days. There may be two broods a year. The chicks forage for insects and green food, and this diet can be supplied in a mixture for chickens available from specialized shops. It can be supplemented by boiled eggs, mealworm larvae and white bread soaked in milk. The newly hatched young must avoid wet ground. When young cocks can be distinguished, they have to be separated from the adult birds.

Adult pheasants are fed maize, barley or oats, soyabean groats, wheat bran, minerals and green food. Reeve's Pheasant can withstand the European winter and may be kept outdoors if a shelter has been provided.

This large species inhabits the mountains of central and northern China, where it ascends to heights of 2,000 metres. It lives in small groups on the margins of woods with bushy undergrowth. In the nesting season, each male (1) usually mates with two hens (2) and protects his territory and partners from rival cocks of the same species.

The first Reeve's Pheasants were imported to Europe in 1831 and they were first bred in England. Successful

breeding, however, dates from as late as 1867. Since then, they have become popular aviary birds in all the countries of Europe. Crossbreeding has been tried with almost every pheasant species, but the hybrids are usually sterile.

Golden Pheasant

Chrysolophus pictus

Phasianidae

This species is one of the most beautiful and least demanding ornamental pheasants. It can be kept throughout the year in a roomy outdoor aviary or freely in the garden. If it is to be kept loose, the primaries on one wing should be trimmed approximately by half. A shelter or hut should be provided for the birds to roost in in winter. The diet consists of wheat, rice, millet, maize, germinating oats, green food, berries and mashed boiled potatoes with groats. In view of the male's excessive sexual activity in the courtship period, one cock should have three to four hens. A courting male struts around the female with his neck collar spread, and makes hissing sounds. The hen builds a sparsely lined nest in thick grass or under a bush. She will also use an artificial nest. The female lays six to sixteen creamy white eggs and incubates them for 22 to 23 days. The chicks are chestnut-brown above with dark streaking, and creamy yellow below. The sides of the head are yellow with dark spots, and there are pale stripes on the dark wings. The young are looked after by the hen. They need a lot of insects, which they can find if kept outdoors. This diet should be supplemented with soft foods rich in animal proteins, including egg mixture, curds, powdered fish or meat, and dried may-flies.

Besides the basic species (1, 2), there are two colour varieties, the yellow Golden Pheasant (3) and the dark Golden Pheasant. The latter has a distinctly darker coloration than the basic species. Crossbreeding a dark pheasant with a normal one produces chicks featuring both colorations.

At the age of one month, young cocks have pale circles around the eyes. Their eyes later turn grey. They have a rust-brown crest, and the plumage is brownish, with dark spots and a yellow sheen. They assume their adult coloration in the second year of age. Young hens have dark brown eyes and lack the hint of spurs.

The Golden Pheasant frequents forest clearings, rocky slopes and bamboo thickets in the mountains of western China. Its habitats are inaccessible and unsuitable for agriculture, and its existence is consequently not imminently threatened. In the wild this species is monogamous. The male (1, 3) measures 100 to 110 centimetres with the tail. The female (2) is 64 to 67 centimetres long. The Chinese kept Golden Pheasants as ornamental birds thousands of years ago.

1 ♂

2 ♀

Lady Amherst's Pheasant

Chrysolophus amherstiae

Phasianidae

Males of this species were first brought to Europe in 1928 by the wife of the British governor in India, Lady Amherst, and the bird was named after her. Breeding was immediately attempted in Europe, but due to the lack of hens the males were crossbred with the females of the Golden Pheasant. The hybrids were fertile, and so this experiment has had lasting consequences: both species still feature undesirable colour ingredients. Breeders are now trying to stabilize the pure populations.

Lady Amherst's Pheasants are fed on wheat, rice, millet, maize, green food, potatoes, beets, and similar substances. In a garden, the hens build a simple nest in a tangle of vegetation. In an aviary they should be provided with an artificial nest with a roof of coniferous branches. The clutch averages fifteen to twenty eggs and the hen sits on it for 23 to 24 days. The chicks resemble the Golden Pheasant's young, but they are slightly bigger and more russet and yellow in colour. They are given a nourishing mixture of grated hard-boiled eggs with grated carrots, curds, dried mayflies, breadcrumbs and powdered fish or meat. At the age of 30 days, young males are distinguished by their grey eye circle and iris. They assume their adult coloration after two years. Adult birds can be kept outdoors throughout the year, but for the winter months they should be provided with a shelter for roosting.

The male (1) reaches a length of 140 to 170 centimetres, while the hen (2) measures 66 to 70 centimetres. The males are aggressive towards the hens, and four to five hens with one male are therefore advisable for an aviary. If the birds are kept freely in a garden with their wings clipped, a male can have two to three hens, but the rear part of the garden should be planted with thick vegetation. To prevent the females from being injured, some breeders file the male's beak and spurs. A courting male jumps over the hen and spreads his neck wings (3).

The home of Lady Amherst's Pheasant is the mountains of western China, south-eastern Tibet and northern Burma. It inhabits margins of forests and high-situated bamboo jungles.

2 ♀

Silver Pheasant

Gennaeus nycthemerus

Phasianidae

The Chinese worshipped the Silver Pheasant as a deity as early as 3,000 BC. It has been bred in England and France since the eighteenth century. Nowadays, it is a semi-domesticated bird, very undemanding, and the most suitable pheasant species for the beginner.

The Silver Pheasant must be kept in a spacious aviary, or with clipped wings in a garden. It is a hardy bird and needs no shelter even in hard winters. It can be fed boiled potatoes, grated carrots, dry bread, ground-meat leftovers and crushed bones. One male should have two to four hens. A nestbox lined with straw and hay should be placed in the aviary. In the garden, the hens make their own nesting hollow in dense vegetation and line it with leaves. The clutch numbers eight to ten, exceptionally up to twenty, eggs. The hen sits on them steadily and reliably for 25 to 26 days. She is a suitable substitute mother for rare species of pheasant. The newly hatched chicks are dark brown above with two longitudinal stripes on the flanks; the head is golden-brown with a fine eye band; the abdomen is yellowish and the feet reddish. The young are fed a nourishing mixture (grated hard-boiled eggs with grated carrots, curds, dried mayflies, breadcrumbs, powdered fish or meat) and finely chopped green food. When kept freely, the chicks pick up insects, worms and snails. After 8 weeks, their diet should be supplemented with barley, hulled oats, wheat and crushed maize. At the age of 12 months, young males develop a blue-black crest and have to be separated from the adults.

3

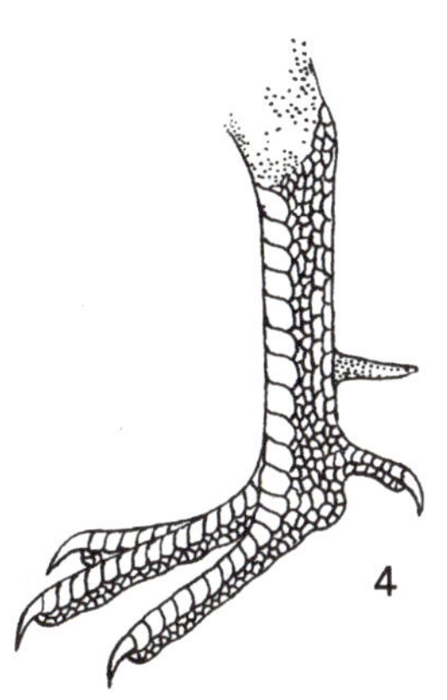

The male (1) attains a length of 120 to 125 centimetres of which about 60 to 70 centimetres is the tail. He has large spurs on the legs (4). The female (2) reaches a length of 70 centimetres including the tail which is 28 centimetres long.

The Silver Pheasant occurs in the mountain forest regions of Burma, Thailand, Vietnam, Laos, Cambodia, southern China and on the island of Hainan. Thirteen geographical forms (subspecies) are recognized. The birds seek mostly the margins of dense mountain forests and bamboo jungles. They prefer heights from 1,500 to 2,000 metres. Their diet is composed of seeds, berries, shoots, young leaves, insects, worms, snails, and so on. They gather in small groups made up of one male and two to five hens. The hens have a hierarchical system. When the hens are sitting on their eggs (3), the male walks around and watches over them.

1 ♂

2 ♀

Indian Peafowl

Pavo cristatus

Phasianidae

The Indian Peafowl is suitable only for larger gardens and parks, where it is kept outdoors throughout the year. A courting male tolerates no rivals in the vicinity. He is polygamous and can have two to five hens, which build nests in thick vegetation under a bush. They also readily accept large hollow tree trunks put in the garden. The clutch of three to five eggs is incubated by the female for 28 days. The female also looks after the young. The chicks have a fawn front part to the mantle and a chestnut-brown rear, and the underparts are buff. They are served grated curds, egg mixture, chopped nettles, milfoil, dandelions and a large quantity of insects. The diet is later supplemented with ground, boiled beef or substituted with the nourishing mixture given to chickens and young turkeys. Adult Peafowl are fed barley, wheat, oats, buckwheat and maize, and occasionally soft foods such as boiled potatoes, groats, grated carrots and sweet potatoes. In large gardens and parks, they forage in the morning and evening for natural food.

At night, Peafowl roost in trees and sometimes on roofs, always in the same spot. The most frequent colour mutation is the white form, which is impressive in the rich greenery of bushes and trees. The other mutations are the multicoloured and black-winged forms.

An adult male (1) measures 180 to 230 centimetres including the elongated feathers above the tail, which are 130 to 160 centimetres long. The hen is 90 to 100 centimetres long (2). The train is composed of up to 150 feathers with eye-like spots (3). A courting male spreads his train and erects it and his tail feathers in a fan-like shape, vertically.

From the back, two black spots and a snow-white spot of down can be seen in the centre.

Indian Peafowl occur in India and Sri Lanka, where they seek predominantly sparse, clear forests. Outside the nesting season they merge in groups made up of birds of both sexes and various ages, even with several adult males in one flock. In the wild they live on berries, seeds, insects, small vertebrates and reptiles. When flushed, they usually run, taking to the air only when in danger.

1 ♂

Crested Pigeon
Ocyphaps lophotes

Columbidae

The Crested Pigeon is native to Australia, occurring throughout most of the continent with the exception of the south-west, south-east and the northernmost tropical part. It has been acclimatized to Europe and in winter can be kept in a garden aviary fitted with a roof. If kept indoors, it should be placed in a spacious cage or in a room equipped as an aviary.

Crested Pigeons eat wheat, millet, hulled oats and chopped green food. This diet is occasionally supplemented with hemp seeds, mainly in winter. The birds must be regularly given clean drinking water.

Hardy deciduous shrubs, such as box-tree or spindle-tree, are planted in the aviary for the Crested Pigeons to nest in. If no live greenery is available, shallow woven baskets can be placed in the branches. The birds must be given birch rods and straw stalks to build their nest. The female lays two glossy eggs 32 by 23 millimetres large. She incubates them alone as a rule, only exceptionally being relieved by the male, who during this time keeps bringing more building material for the nest. The eggs are incubated for 18 days, and the chicks are fed for 3 weeks on the nest. Some 15 days after fledging, they are still fed by their parents. As soon as they become independent, they should be transferred to another aviary because the adult male will start to pursue them.

Both sexes (1) are alike in coloration, and their crest makes them visually remarkable from a distance. Each wing shows the characteristic turquoise speculum (2). The feet have, typically, short tarsi and long toes (3).

In their Australian homeland, Crested Pigeons nest in spring or early summer, or after the rainy season. The flat, flimsy nest measures about 170 millimetres across and is usually situated some 3 metres above the ground. It is built in forked branches or split trees, often in dense foliage. Flying pigeons make metallic sounds with their flapping wings.

The luring call is quiet and wavering, while the alarm call is noisy and explosive. A courting male produces an unusual blunt 'woomp . . . woomp . . .' sound, while he lifts and dips his head and spreads his wings and tail.

Diamond Dove Columbidae
Geopelia cuneata

This miniature dove reaches a length of only 19 to 22 centimetres. It is very undemanding and therefore well suited for keeping, preferably in a garden or indoor aviary. If kept in a cage the female will lay eggs, but usually leaves the clutch. In a heated aviary, the doves can be left outdoors throughout the winter, for they have adapted remarkably well to the European climate.

Diamond Doves nest readily in an aviary with thick vegetation cover, and are often used to rear some rare species of dove. The courting male is extremely animated, and will bow before the female, holding his tail feathers upright in a fan-like shape. The birds either build their own nest or use a provided small flat basket or box. Hay, straw and short, thin willow twigs must be supplied as building materials. The clutch consists of two smooth white eggs 20 by 16 millimetres large. Incubation is carried out by both partners. The young hatch after 13 days, grow rapidly and leave the nest when they are 10 days old. The diet is canary seed, millet, poppyseed, Senegal millet in ears, finely chopped green food and egg mixture. It does not have to be supplemented while the young are fed.

Several pairs can be kept together only if the aviary is sufficiently large because the males fight. Diamond Doves can, however, be kept together with other small species of birds.

Some practice is needed to distinguish the sexes. The brown coloration in the female is usually darker than in the male (1). In its Australian homeland, the Diamond Dove is one of the most extraordinary birds. In summer, during the midday heat

1 ♂

when the temperature surpasses 45 degrees Centigrade in the shade, all the other birds experience difficulty and will shelter under eucalyptus trees, with wings hung down and open beaks. Diamond Doves, on the other hand, sit on the scorching sand, the temperature of which reaches 70 degrees Centigrade, ruffle their feathers, and lift the wings to expose their bodies to the Sun's rays. It is thus surprising how well they have adjusted to European conditions in captivity. A drinking Diamond Dove assumes a characteristic posture with its body conspicuously stretched (2). Breeders recognize three varieties: grey, silver and grey-white.

Bleeding-heart Pigeon
Gallicolumba luzonica

Columbidae

This beautiful pigeon, up to 26 centimetres long, can be kept in a garden during the summer but must be kept in an indoor aviary for the rest of the year. The winter temperature must not drop below freezing point as this species' legs are very susceptible to frostbite. It requires the largest possible space because it is hostile to other species of birds and often attacks even other members of its own species.

In the wild, the Bleeding-heart Pigeon lives in forests, moving predominantly on the ground where it forages for seeds, fruits and insects. In captivity, it requires a different diet from that given to other pigeons. In addition to wheat, millet and vetch, it has to be served egg mixture, boiled rice, oatflakes, grated boiled potatoes and hard curds. Apples and pears cut into small pieces are added throughout the year, and chickweed, duckweed, lettuce, dandelion and the like are supplemented in season.

For nesting, Bleeding-heart Pigeons need dense shrubs in which they build an ungainly nest from birch and willow twigs and from straw provided by the keeper. They prefer to settle in shallow baskets or wooden platforms, which should be hung some 1 to 1.5 metres above the ground. The clutch comprises two eggs which hatch in 15 to 17 days. Successful rearing of the young depends on nourishment, and the food should at that time be enriched by ant cocoons, mealworm larvae, small snails and insects collected in a meadow. Young pigeons leave the nest after 14 to 15 days. They spend the first day moving on the ground and later roost in the branches.

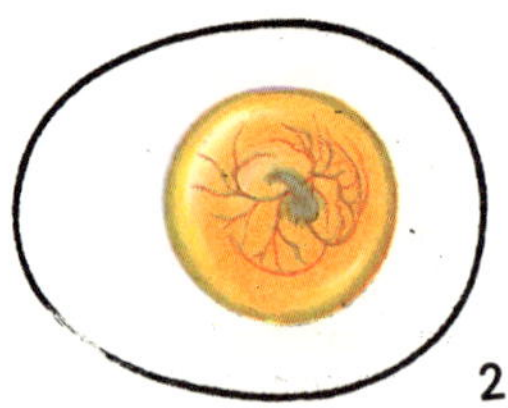

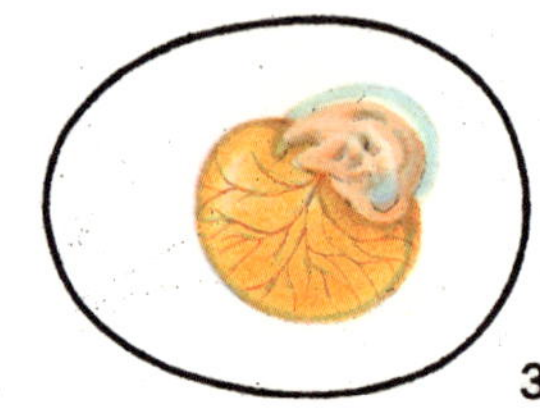

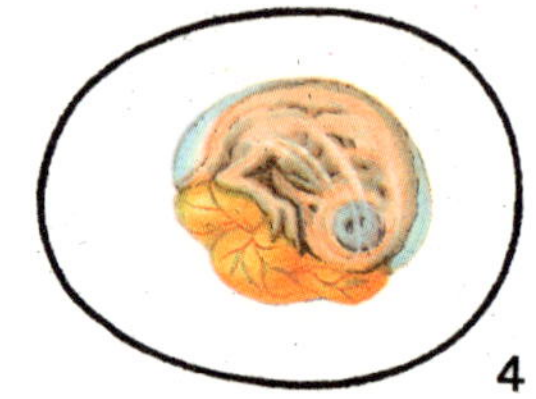

The subspecies *G. l. luzonica* inhabits the Philippine Islands of Luzon and Polillo. The subspecies *G. l. crinigera* is restricted to the island of Mindanao; it is biologically interesting because it always lays a single egg. Both sexes in the Bleeding-heart Pigeon are identically coloured (1). The male can be recognized by his interesting courting ritual. He slowly dips and lifts his head at brief intervals and erects his tail feathers.

In captivity, the parent birds sometimes stop feeding their young, probably because of the substitute food. Some breeders put their eggs under an incubating Turtle Dove (*Streptopelia turtur*) or a domestic pigeon. It is, however, rather difficult to get the foster parents used to animal food.

The cross section of an egg shows the development of an embryo at: 3 days (2), 7 days (3), 10 days (4), 2 weeks (5).

Cape Dove
Oena capensis

Columbidae

Outdoor aviaries are best suited for breeding the beautiful Cape Doves, which should, however, stay there only in spring and summer. They are sensitive to low temperatures and high humidity, and they have to spend winter in heated quarters. Shrubs can be planted in the outdoor aviary, where the doves can build a flimsy nest composed of thin layers of grass, twigs and roots. When sounding its 'coo-coo', the Cape Dove stresses and prolongs the second syllable. The courting male pursues his mate, bows, spreads his tail and calls 'cook'. He often feeds the female from his crop. In the nesting period, Cape Doves should be kept in single pairs, although they get along well with small songbirds of the genus *Ploceus.* Some pairs do not tolerate being disturbed by either the keeper or other species of birds and leave the clutch. If the aviary lacks shrubs suitable for nesting, a box or a bunch of twigs can be placed in the aviary as a building platform. The female usually lays two dull-cream, rough-shelled eggs and incubates them for 14 to 15 days. The young grow rapidly and leave the nest after 12 days. Twenty-two days after fledging, the males show a black pattern on the head, and after 7 weeks start growing black feathers on the breast. They have adult coloration at the age of 6 months.

Adult Cape Doves are fed millet, canary seed, poppyseed, hulled oats, egg mixture and green foods.

An asset in this 26-centimetre-long dove is the easy distinction of the sexes. The male (1) has a strikingly black front area on the head and throat, while in the female (2) this part of the body is a dull brown colour, and her forehead is pale. The subspecies *O. c. capensis* is found (with the exception of Central African primary forests) in the territory ranging from Morocco and the Sudan to South Africa and Saudi Arabia. The second subspecies, *O. c. aliena,* lives in Madagascar.

The habitat of the Cape Dove is open country covered with scrub and forest-steppes. In some areas, the Cape Dove nests in city parks or villages. In the wild, the nesting season depends on the availability of food. The nest is usually situated very low down, often less than 50 centimetres above the ground in a bush (3).

Rainbow Lorikeet
Trichoglossus haematodus

Loriidae

This lorikeet is probably the most frequently kept species from the family Loriidae. It is popular for its magnificent plumage, and because it breeds freely in captivity and withstands inclement weather. It is undemanding in terms of food, especially some subspecies. Imported birds quickly get used to sunflower seeds, canary seed, oats and other cereals. The diet must be supplemented with honey, sweetened milk, fruit juices and other substitute foods suitable for lorikeets. They consume a lot of apples, carrots, and in season appreciate grapes. Newly imported birds are kept at room temperature, but after acclimatization they are resistant to sudden weather changes. In winter, they should be transferred to a frostproof room. Rainbow Lorikeets are usually kept in pairs, but they also get along well with Budgerigars. Their call is subdued and they are vocally silent as a rule, except when alarmed and flushed.

Rainbow Lorikeets are adaptable in nesting. Although they prefer natural cavities, they will make do with an artificial nestbox with an entry hole 8 centimetres across. The bottom of the nestbox must be covered with a thickish layer of peat mixed with sawdust. The birds use the nestbox at night as well, so it has to be cleaned regularly.

They are very quiet in the nesting period. The female lays two white eggs and incubates them for 23 to 25 days. The young are fed by both parents and leave the nest after 7 to 8 weeks.

The sexes are identical in coloration, except for the iris, which is bright red in the male and orange-reddish in the female. Juvenile birds resemble their parents, but their tail feathers are shorter and the beaks are less red.

The Rainbow Lorikeet has an extensive area of distribution covering New Guinea, Bali, the Solomon Islands, New Hebrides, New Caledonia, northern and eastern Australia and Tasmania. Twenty-one subspecies are recognized which differ substantially in coloration. The best-known subspecies, *T. h. mollucanus* (1), inhabits eastern and southern Australia; *T. h. rubritorquis* (2) is distributed in northern Australia, *T. h. haematodus* (3) lives on the islands of Buru, Amboina, Ceram, Ceramlaut, Goram, Watubela, in western Papua and west of New Guinea; and *T. h. weberi* (4) occurs on the island of Flores. The underparts of the wings of *T. h. mollucanus* (5) show the features distinguishing it from *T. h. rubritorquis*, whose wings are red above, with a wide yellow edge.

1
2
3
4

Blue-tailed Lory
Lorius lory

The plumage of lories is characterized by a broad colour range, and they rank among the most beautiful parrots. They have special brush-like tongues with fleshy tubular tips adapted for taking liquid food, such as from flowers, and the juice of tropical fruits, as well as soft fruit and tiny insects. In captivity, their natural foods have to be replaced by honey, sweetened milk, syrup, sweetened fruit pulp and juice, custard, soaked sponge, and liquid rice or maize flour pudding. They require soft fruit such as bananas, oranges and strawberries, which in winter can be substituted by tinned fruit. Unripe maize ears can be served in season. Lories also eat mealworm larvae, ant cocoons, hard-boiled eggs, raw yolks with cream and honey, curds and meat stock. Only some lories welcome green food, and they rarely get used to millet, oats and sunflower seeds. The Blue-tailed Lory finds it difficult to feed on cereals.

The birds can be kept singly or in pairs. They prefer indoor aviaries but can spend the summer in a large outdoor aviary with a sheltered section. The temperature must never fall below 10 degrees Centigrade. For nesting, large hollow trunks or wooden boxes at least 130 centimetres long should be provided and hung on the walls. The clutch of two eggs is incubated by the female for 24 days.

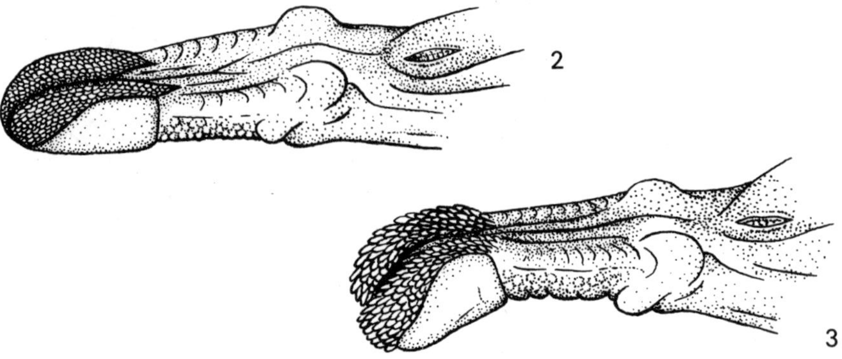

The Blue-tailed Lory (1) is about 31 centimetres long. The sexes are alike. The young lack the red band on the neck. They have a green mantle, red upper breast and greenish lower coverts mixed with blue and red feathers. If kept separately, a Blue-tailed Lory is very affectionate and gifted. It learns to whistle short tunes and to imitate sounds and words. Once the owner establishes a regular feeding system, the seemingly complicated preparations become simple.

This species occurs in seven subspecies in the primary forests of New Guinea and Papua. It is a hole-nester and excellent flier. The tip of the tongue is normally contracted (2), the tubes opening only when the bird takes food (3).

Lesser Sulphur-crested Cockatoo

Cacatua sulphurea

Cacatuidae

This is the most frequently imported species of cockatoo. When well treated, it soon becomes tame and affectionate to its owner. It learns easily and can repeat words, tunes and imitate other birds. If kept singly in a room, it should be allowed to move freely outside the cage. From spring to autumn, these cockatoos can be put in outdoor aviaries provided with a shelter. In summer, they enjoy exposing their bodies to the rain, stretching their wings and getting soaked. In the winter months, they should stay in a room at a temperature of about 10 degrees Centigrade. The diet is the same as in other cockatoos: sunflower seeds, maize, oats, nuts, various fruits, hard-boiled eggs, white bread, insects, and so on.

The courting male hops around the female and bends to the ground to the accompaniment of luring sounds. He also erects his crest and both birds ruffle one another's feathers. The clutch of two to three eggs is usually incubated by the male during the day and by the female at night. Incubation takes 25 days and the young stay in the nest for further 2 months. During this period, the diet should be supplemented with raisins, unripe wheat, pea pods, dry bread soaked in sweetened milk, or with mealworm larvae. The newly fledged young resemble the adult birds except in having white beaks and feet. If the female starts plucking the chicks' feathers, more protein should be added to the food, for example, by serving curds. If kept with care, cockatoos live in captivity for dozens of years.

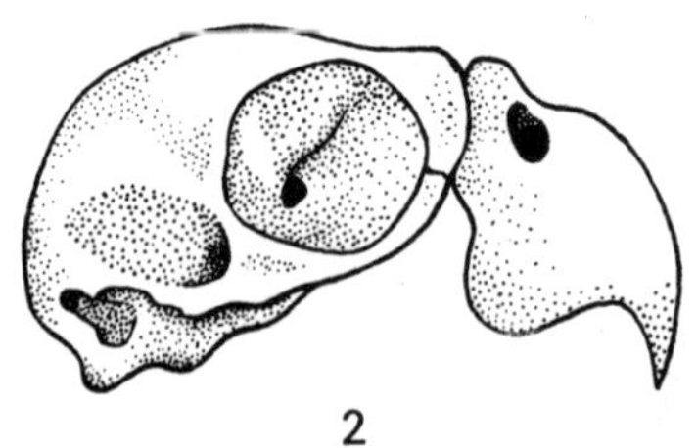

The sexes in the Lesser Sulphur-crested Cockatoo (1) are distinguished by the eye-colour, those of the male being blackish-brown and those of the female reddish-brown. Juvenile birds have pale beaks and feet. When being fed, they flutter their wings, and some 2 weeks after hatching they begin to peck up the food brought by the parents. As soon as the adult birds show interest in rearing a second brood, they start chasing the young away and these have to be transferred to another aviary.

An adult cockatoo reaches a length of 35 centimetres, with a wing length of 24 centimetres, and the tail measures 11 centimetres. The upper mandible is conspicuously massive (2). This species is distributed in six subspecies throughout the Indonesian Archipelago.

Sulphur-crested Cockatoo
Cacatua galerita

The Sulphur-crested Cockatoo is a large white cockatoo with a bold, yellow crest. It is about 49 centimetres long, 21 centimetres of this being the tail. A young cockatoo can be easily tamed and taught to repeat sentences, whistle tunes and skilfully mimic sounds. Its natural voice is a harsh croaking. It soon becomes affectionate and is usually kept singly.

If breeding is to be attempted, the birds have to be housed in a large all-wire aviary provided with a shelter. For nesting, they need large hollow trunks, only exceptionally settling in a wooden nestbox. If possible, it is advisable to get more than two birds, and allow them to choose their partners themselves. The female lays two elliptical eggs measuring 47 by 37 millimetres in a nesting cup lined with decaying wood. The clutch is incubated by both parents for 30 days, the male sitting on it during the day and the female at night. The young stay in the nesting cavity for 6 to 11 weeks. After fledging, they look like their parents, except for the nape, mantle and wings, which have a greyish sheen.

The Sulphur-crested Cockatoo requires the same diet as other species of cockatoo. It needs a lot of fruit and prefers sunflower seeds to all the cereals. Minerals are added to egg mixture, especially when the young are being fed, and the diet is at that time supplemented with boiled barley, strawberries, carrots, radishes, hemp seeds, and so on.

The Sulphur-crested Cockatoo normally has its crest folded on the nape (2), opening it in a fan-like shape when disturbed (3). The female has the same coloration as the male but her iris is usually red-brown, while that of the male is black.

2

3

In the wild, it occurs in four subspecies. *C. g. galerita* (1) inhabits south-eastern Australia and Tasmania; *C. g. fitzroyi* lives in northern Australia: *C. g. triton* is found in New Guinea, the Trobriand Islands, and on the islands of Ceramlaut and Goramlaut; and the smallest subspecies, *C. g. eleonora,* is confined to the island of Aru in the Indonesian Archipelago. In these regions, the Sulphur-crested Cockatoo lives mainly on eucalyptus fruits, berries, nuts, fruit, roots, insects and their larvae. In the southern areas, it nests from August to January, and in the northern tropics from May to September.

Salmon-crested Cockatoo

Cacatua moluccensis

Cacatuidae

The Salmon-crested Cockatoo is one of the largest and most beautiful cockatoos. Its total length is 50 centimetres, the wing measures 31 centimetres and the tail is 17 centimetres long. It has a distinct crest, with a length of up to 18 centimetres. When excited, it erects the crest and the feathers on the neck, nape and breast, forming a kind of collar. The Salmon-crested Cockatoo is very docile. A tame specimen soon learns to reproduce words, whistle tunes or imitate familiar sounds. A newly imported bird sometimes makes unpleasant shrieking noises. To stop this the cage can be covered with a dark cloth.

Newly imported cockatoos are placed in large all-wire cages where they can stretch their wings but cannot fly. When well treated, they soon become tame and very pleasant companions. They are undemanding and hardy. With their powerful beaks, they often chip thin planks to pieces, and they should be provided with fresh tree branches to file the beaks on.

The Salmon-crested Cockatoo is usually kept singly. Breeding can be attempted in large all-wire aviaries with a shelter, where the birds can stay from spring to autumn. In winter, they are transferred to an indoor aviary or other room, where the temperature should not drop below zero. It usually nests in hollow tree trunks. If these are not available, a nestbox should be provided, 150 centimetres high with a base 50 by 50 centimetres. The entry hole should be large, roughly 17 to 20 centimetres across. A part of one wall or the lid should be adjusted to facilitate inspection of the nest. The clutch of three to four eggs is incubated by the female alone for 35 days. The young look like their parents except for the absence of the pinkish sheen, which they acquire only after 1 to 2 years.

The mainstay of the Salmon-crested Cockatoo's diet is sunflower, oats, maize, nuts and plenty of fruit. Minerals and vitamins must be supplemented regularly.

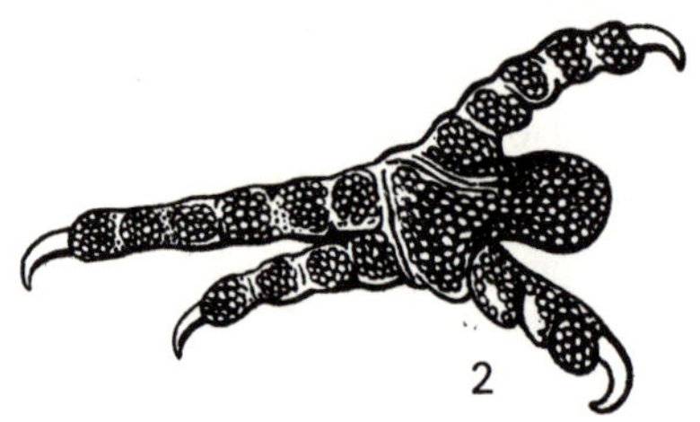

The sexes can be distinguished with great difficulty; the female has allegedly a more delicate pink sheen, yellowish tail feathers and a narrower head.

In the wild, the Salmon-crested Cockatoo (1) occurs in the southern part of the Moluccas on the islands of Seram,

Saparua, Haruku and Amboina. It flies expertly and noiselessly in the crowns of tall trees. Its feet (2) are sophisticated tools serving to hold food or to open the door of the cage. The lower side of the upper mandible is conspicuously notched (3).

Greater White-crested Cockatoo

Cacatuidae

Cacatua alba

This beautiful white cockatoo is kept very rarely. Some bird-keepers or zoological gardens keep these birds on metal perches, loosely chained by a foot. This is the wrong way to keep a cockatoo; it should be tamed instead. Newly imported cockatoos are shy and restless. They should be placed in rather small but solid cages. The owner has to keep the birds company, avoiding sudden movements and catching them in hand. They soon become tame and affectionate, learning to whistle tunes or imitate various sounds.

The crest is the most eminent feature in cockatoos; it becomes erect when the birds are disturbed, and otherwise remains folded. An adult cockatoo is 40 to 45 centimetres long, the wing measures 30 centimetres and the tail is 18 centimetres long.

The diet is composed of sunflower seed, maize, oats, wheat, nuts, fruit, carrots, dandelion, chickweed, and so on. The Greater White-crested Cockatoo likes to bite wood and fresh branches have to be supplied.

Some bird-keepers have been trying to breed this species in large aviaries. The best size for nestboxes is 50 by 40 by 50 centimetres, but natural nests in hollow trees are preferred. The two to four white eggs are incubated by both parents for roughly a month. When feeding the young, cockatoos have to be given egg mixture, curd, minerals, insects, mealworm larvae, and so on. The young remain dependent on their parents for a long lime after they fledge. In the nesting period even well-tamed cockatoos become aggressive.

The Greater White-crested Cockatoo (1) has the same life expectancy as humans. The sexes are difficult to distinguish as the distinctive traits are unreliable. When several birds are kept together, their sexes can be found out by watching their behaviour. Sometimes the sexes can be recognized by the eye, that of the male being black while the female's iris is reddish-brown.

The Greater White-crested Cockatoo is imported from the northern and central Moluccas and from the islands of Halmahera, Obi, Batjan, Ternate and Tidore, where it lives in forest areas. When drinking, cockatoos often like to stand in the water and soak their underparts (2).

1 ♂

Cockatiel

Cacatuidae

Nymphicus hollandicus

Next to the Budgerigar, the Cockatiel is the most popular Australian parrot. It is very undemanding, hardy, and breeds well in captivity. The birds can be kept in a large cage or indoor aviary, but preferably should be in an outdoor aviary with a shelter, where they can stay throughout the year.

Cockatiels are fed sunflower seed, canary seed, oats, various kinds of millet, sliced carrots, apples and other fruit, plantain spikelets and chickweed. They must be given fresh twigs to nibble on. When the adults are feeding their young, the diet should include germinating setaria, egg mixture and soaked white bread.

The nestbox may be either natural or made from planks. It should be 35 to 40 centimetres high and 20 centimetres deep and wide, and the entry hole should have a diameter of 8 to 9 centimetres. Cockatiels have up to three broods a year, which can prove harmful to the parents' health. The clutch comprises four to seven white eggs which are incubated by the male during the day and by the female at night for 16 to 21 days. The young are fed in the nest for 4 to 5 weeks and for another 3 to 4 weeks after they have fledged. Juvenile birds resemble the female, but their flesh-coloured beaks become dark only after some 3 months. Male cockatiels which are kept singly can be easily tamed, while females rarely become entirely tame. The birds learn to alight on the owner's shoulder or finger and to imitate tunes, sounds and words.

The male (1) differs slightly from the female (2) in colour. Many colour variants have been bred. The first white Cockatiels (5) were bred in the United States in 1959, and the Californian multi-coloured Cockatiels of the same year (4) were later followed by pearl-coloured (3), cinnamon and other variants.

This species is widespread in Australia except in the coastal regions. Huge flocks of Cockatiels live in open steppes, savannahs and pastureland. They form pairs within the flocks and stay together even when covering long distances. When drought in some parts of their nesting territory results in food shortages, the flocks are forced to migrate in search of food and water.

Eclectus Parrot
Eclectus roratus

Psittacidae

Males and females of this magnificent parrot were in the past believed to be two different species. They had been known for almost 100 years when in 1874 Dr A. B. Meyer, director of the Museum of Natural History in Munich, explained their striking and unusual sexual dimorphism. There are even vocal differences between the sexes: the male's 'krraach-krraak' is heard mainly in the courtship period, the female's voice sounds like 'khe-ong . . .khe-ong'. The Eclectus Parrot is a quiet bird, and is easy to tame even when older.

Newly imported birds find it difficult to acclimatize and they have to be kept at room temperature. They are served fresh maize ears, and during acclimatization they need boiled maize and rice, both dry and germinating sunflower seeds, ripe fruit of all kinds, carrots, sponge, hips, rowanberries, grapes, snowberries, chickweed, lettuce and dandelion flowers. They drink a lot of water and spraying with tepid water is highly beneficial.

There is a growing interest in breeding Eclectus Parrots, because they multiply well in captivity. They should be kept in an aviary in which the temperature is kept above zero by heating. A number of branches are placed in it. The nestbox should be 30 by 30 by 45 centimetres, the entry hole 10 centimetres across, and the bottom should be covered with an 8-centimetre-high layer of wood pulp. Nesting begins by an interesting courtship. The clutch is composed of two eggs which are incubated by the female while the male brings her food. The young fledge after 8 weeks and return to the hole for several more weeks.

The male (1) is markedly different from the female (2). The sexes in the young can be easily distinguished also; juvenile males (3) are green and females (4) are red. Only the upper mandible in young birds is dark brownish-grey, the tip being a dirty yellow. The iris of their eyes is brownish. The massive upper mandible is very pronounced on the flat skull (5).

The Eclectus Parrot occurs in twelve subspecies in the Moluccas, Lesser Sunda Islands, and in the islands of Tanimbar, Aru, Kai and New Guinea; in Australia it inhabits the York Peninsula, Bismarck

Archipelago, Solomon Islands, and Goram and Palau. It frequents dense primary forests, often in mountainous areas. On some islands, Eclectus Parrots live in coconut palm groves, feeding on the fruit. They are solitary, seeking mates only in the breeding season.

King Parrot
Alisterus scapularis

Psittacidae

These handsome parrots must be kept in large and very long outdoor aviaries, fitted with only a few branches, to give the birds ample space to fly around. After acclimatization, King Parrots can withstand European winters in a sheltered part of the aviary. Their diet is simple, mainly sunflower seed, oats, maize, wheat, setaria, peanuts, carrots, apples and other fruit, and green food.

King Parrots do not breed easily in captivity. For nesting, they should be offered at least two hollows, preferably in a tree trunk about 100 to 200 centimetres long and 30 centimetres in diameter, with an entry hole 10 centimetres across. At the beginning of the nesting season, the female asks to be fed by the male, and the diet has to be supplemented with crumbled biscuits or white bread, chopped hard-boiled eggs, fresh seeds and various weeds, germinating seeds and maize, sponge, and so on. The courting male erects his head feathers, bends forward, contracts the pupils of his eyes, jerks his wings to the accompaniment of strange grating sounds. The female lays four to five white eggs measuring 33 by 26 milimetres and incubates them for 19 to 21 days. The young leave the nest at the age of 5 to 6 weeks. King Parrots bred in captivity can become very tame and affectionate if well looked after, while imported birds, especially adults, can rarely be tamed.

King Parrots reach a length of 43 centimetres. The male (1) is sexually mature at 3 years of age, while the female (2) usually matures after 2 years. Juvenile birds (3) resemble the female. Young females are brown-eyed. After a year, young males show a pale green band on the upper side of the wings.

King Parrots inhabit eastern and south-eastern coastal areas of Australia, extending from northern Queensland to southern Victoria. They seek wooded

locations with dense undergrowth. In some national parks where they are never disturbed, they approach people without fear. On large farms they feed together with poultry. They build nests in hollow branches or in the trunks of eucalyptus trees and retain their breeding capacity for more than thirty years.

Princess Parrot

Polytelis alexandrae

The Princess Parrot, a delicate-pastel bird, is kept usually in an outdoor aviary. It is neither wild nor shy, but it cannot be confined to a cage because of its long tail feathers. If given ample space, it will display its beauty in flight. Wood can be used for the frame of the aviary since the Princess Parrot does not bite wood. No heating is necessary in the shelter, since the birds can withstand freezing weather. Two pairs can be housed in a large aviary, or one pair in the company of a Cockatiel or Bourke's Parrot. A pair nesting alone will, however, rear a better brood.

Princess Parrots are fed millet, canary seed, hulled and unhulled oats, wheat, sunflower seed, various small weed seeds, apples, carrots, chickweed, and so on. Plenty of germinating grain and egg mixture should be supplied in the breeding season. Princess Parrots usually peck the germinating seeds from the ground and may be infected by parasitic worms such as those of the genus *Ascaris*. Concurat or Panacur is used for treatment.

The courtship is very interesting: the male rocks from side to side, hopping around the female and trying to feed her, while contracting his eyes. For nesting, a nestbox, from 50 to 200 centimetres long, is placed in the sheltered part of the aviary; it is hung obliquely to prevent the female from breaking the eggs when she flies in. The clutch numbers four to six eggs. Incubation lasts 20 days and the young are fledged after 5 weeks.

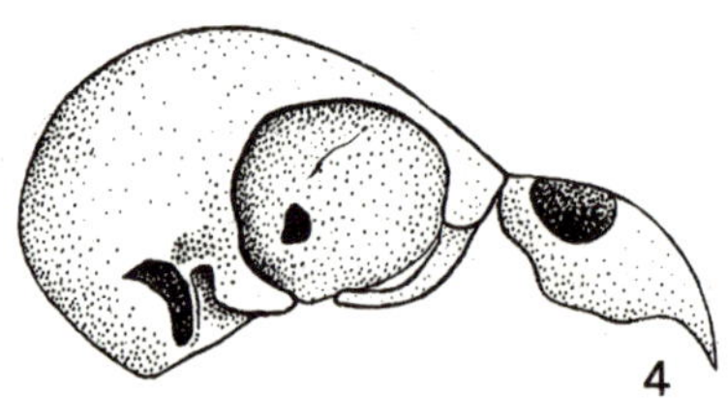

The Princess Parrot reaches a length of 45 centimetres. The male (1) has longer tail feathers than the female and one feather on the third pair of his primaries is elongated by 12 to 14 millimetres. The female (2) lacks this feature, her nape is greyish to pale violet and the green wing feathers are streaked with a dark

olive-green (3). There is a rare blue variety and a recent lutino mutation. The shape of the skull is reminiscent of a riding cap (4).

This species is restricted to the inland regions of western Australia, extending to the northern reaches of southern Australia. It inhabits plains which are often situated far from water. There are few reports of its occurrence in the wild in recent years. When foraging for food, it is extremely quiet, but it is a noisy bird when moving in the forest canopy. It is excellently camouflaged when it presses itself close to a branch.

Crimson Rosella

Platycercus elegans

Psittacidae

This parakeet has gained great popularity with aviculturists due to its beautiful plumage and its hardiness. It is not suited to a cage and should be displayed in an outdoor aviary where it can be kept throughout the year. It often bathes even in freezing weather. It has a pleasant voice which is raised only in the mating season.

Crimson Rosellas feed on sunflower seed, canary seed, oats, wheat, millet, and large quantities of apples, carrots, rowanberries and snowberries, whole dandelions, chickweed and plantain spikelets. Fresh twigs must be supplied for the birds to nibble on.

Early in spring, the male becomes quarrelsome and no other Crimson Rosellas should be kept in an adjacent aviary. The birds are undemanding in selecting a nesting cavity, settling readily in either a natural or artificial nestbox, although the female sits more reliably in a long tree trunk hung on the wall. She lays four to eight creamy white eggs measuring 29 by 24 millimetres. Incubation is 21 days and the young stay in the nest for another 5 weeks. For 2 to 3 weeks after fledging, they are fed by their parents. Juvenile birds are green with a few red feathers on the breast and abdomen. They moult after 13 to 15 months. Undernourished nestlings sometimes become red in the nestbox and remain stunted, while well-fed chicks are strong and leave the nest in green coloration. Some Crimson Rosellas breed in their first year before assuming their adult coloration, although breeding is not advisable in birds under 2 years old. Crimson Rosellas exceptionally rear two broods in a year.

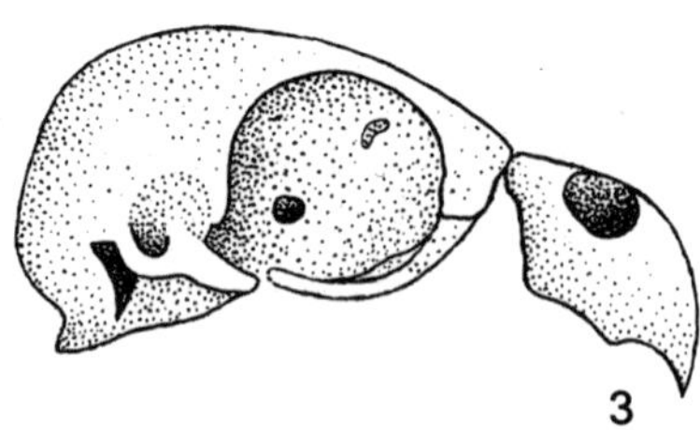

This species attains a length of 32 to 36 centimetres. The female is identical in coloration to the male (1) but she has a smaller head and a narrower base to the beak. The skull (3) has a characteristic protuberance on the lower edge of the occipital bone.

It is native to the coastal areas of eastern and southern Australia. It inhabits large forests and their humidity affects the intensity of the red coloration. The tropical northern regions are inhabited by the subspecies *P.e.nigrescens* whose offspring leave the nest clad in almost red plumage, while in the subspecies *P.e.elegans* and *P.e.melanoptera* the juveniles are green (2). Crimson Rosellas

living in the south have been observed at heights of 2,000 metres in situations covered by snow in the winter. In the wild, their diet consists partly of fruits and seeds of eucalyptus trees and other plants, and partly of insects.

Eastern Rosella Psittacidae
Platycercus eximius

The Eastern Rosella is one of the best species for anyone wishing to start breeding Australian parakeets. It can be kept in a cage, an indoor or an outdoor aviary. This hardy bird thrives best, however, in an outdoor aviary, which need be only 2 metres long. It does not damage wood so that the frame and the sheltered part of the aviary can be made of wood. The Eastern Rosella can be kept singly and the males are easier to tame. It will learn to repeat a few words and sing short tunes in a flute-like voice.

The diet, as for other Autralian parakeets, is sunflower seed, millet, canary seed, oats, carrots, apples, rowanberries and green food. When the parent birds are feeding their young, soaked white bread and egg mixture should be added.

The Eastern Rosella is undemanding as regards the nesting hollow. The nestbox should be about 40 centimetres high and 25 centimetres long, with an entry hole measuring 8 centimetres across. The courting male spreads his tail feathers and shakes them. The clutch numbers four to nine white eggs; the female lays an egg every other day and starts sitting when the third egg is deposited. The young hatch after 20 to 21 days and leave the nest when they are 4 weeks old. The sexes are usually evenly divided. They often rear two broods a year. Breeding of too young birds can prove to be unsuccessful. Many birdkeepers use Eastern Rosellas to rear rare species of parrots.

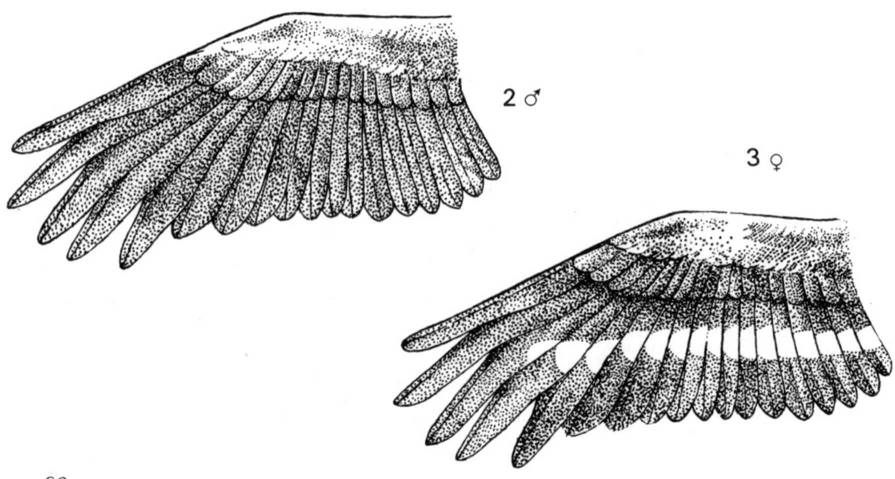

The length of an adult Eastern Rosella is 30 to 32 centimetres. The female resembles the male (1) but has a smaller head, her red coloration is duller and less extensive, and the facial patch is smaller. Juvenile birds have duller plumage and the head and neck are more green than red, the males being stouter and redder on the head than the females. The male usually lacks a band on the wing (2), while in the female the wing shows a pale band on the underside (3).

Two subspecies of the Eastern Rosella are found in south-eastern Australia, while the subspecies *P.e.diemensis* lives in Tasmania. Although it is originally a resident of savannahs, the Eastern Rosella can nowadays be found in parks of large cities and in cultivated areas. It nests in hollow tree trunks, sometimes even low down in stumps.

Pale-headed Rosella

Platycercus adscitus

Psittacidae

A few years ago, European aviculturists regarded the Pale-headed Rosella as a rarity. It has since become a commonly bred and highly popular species of parakeet. It flourishes in an outdoor aviary where no heating is necessary as long as the shelter is dry and protected from draughts.

The diet is sunflower and canary seed, oats, small quantities of hemp seed, setaria, a great deal of weed seeds, chickweed, apples and carrots. When feeding their young, the birds should be served germinating seeds, soaked white bread, egg mixture and more carrots, apples and chickweed.

When preparing for breeding, the male starts feeding the female and she visits the nestbox. Mating occurs early in the morning and late in the evening. The clutch comprises three to eight eggs measuring 27 by 22 millimetres, which are incubated for 22 to 24 days. This species prefers a tall nestbox where the sitting female can have peace and is not disturbed by the male. Some females are very sensitive to disturbance, while others tolerate even frequent inspections of the nest. The Pale-headed Rosella sometimes rears two broods in a year. Young birds mature slowly, leaving the nestbox 32 to 35 days after hatching. Their colours are duller than those of adult birds and the head is an olive-russet colour. They assume their adult coloration at the age of 12 to 15 months. The sexes are easier to distinguish in newly fledged birds than in older juveniles. Young males have a more robust head and a wider beak.

Adult Pale-headed Rosellas attain a length of 33 centimetres and the sexes are almost identical in appearance. The female, however, has a less pronounced pattern on the head and the underparts of her wings show a bold pale band, depicted (3) in the subspecies *P.a.palliceps.*

This species is confined to north-eastern Autralia, extending from the York Peninsula to northern New South Wales. There are two subspecies, the more common *P.a.palliceps* (1), and the smaller *P.a.adscitus* (2), which lives in the York Peninsula. In its natural habitat, the Pale-headed Rosella nests from

February to June. It lives on the fruits of eucalyptus trees and on the blossoms of trees of the genus *Melaleuca.* Its favourite haunts are savannahs, where it forages for a variety of seeds. It also visits fruit plantations and sunflower and maize fields, and will eat insects.

Western Rosella
Platycercus icterotis

The Western Rosella is one of the most popular Australian parakeets. It can be kept in a cage, an outdoor or an indoor aviary. It has a pleasant and unobtrusive flute-like voice and its affectionate, quiet behaviour make it an ideal bird for a beginner. Young birds, especially males, raised by humans become particularly tame.

This species is undemanding as far as feeding is concerned. The diet consists of sunflower seed, various sorts of millet, niger seed, flax seed, oats, wheat, chickweed, seeds of dandelion, plantain and shepherd's-purse, carrots, apples and other fruit. Egg mixture is served when the young are being fed.

The cage or aviary does not have to be too large and the construction can be made of wood because the birds do not destroy it. A shelter must be provided but heating in the winter is not necessary. Juvenile birds sometimes breed at the age of one year, before attaining adult coloration. The nestbox, about 30 to 50 centimetres high, should have a base measuring 25 by 25 centimetres. Some breeders use higher boxes, while others have achieved better results in smaller ones. The clutch numbers three to eight white eggs measuring 26 by 22 millimetres, which are incubated by the female for 21 to 25 days. The young are fed in the nest for 28 to 32 days, sometimes longer. Juvenile males are richer in colour than the females and have bigger heads. Adult coloration is assumed after 12 to 15 months.

The Western Rosella is up to 27 centimetres long. The male (1) differs strikingly in colour from the female (2). Juvenile birds are predominantly green, lack the facial patch, and the future red colour on the abdomen and head is heralded only by a few feathers (3).

In the wild, the Western Rosella is restricted to the south-west of Western Australia. It is a common bird which does not gather in large flocks and consequently does not cause great damage to wheat fields or fruit orchards. Despite their tame behaviour and magnificent red plumage, Western Rosellas are not heavily pursued by man. They are very quiet, especially during the day when they seek shade in the branches of eucalyptus trees. They are active predominantly in the morning and evening, foraging for food. They are not migratory.

Red-rumped Parrot Psittacidae
Psephotus haematonotus

Next to the Budgerigar and the Cockatiel, the Red-rumped Parrot is the most frequently bred aviary species. It is suitable for beginners, and experienced aviculturists use it to rear rare species of parrots of the same or related genus. Another asset is the easy distinction of the sexes even in very young nestlings; young females and males are similar in appearance to their parents, but the colours are more subdued.

The Red-rumped Parrot can be kept in an outdoor aviary throughout the year, withstanding even hard frosts. It can also be placed in a cage about 1 metre long or smaller. There are usually two broods a year; a third one is exceptional. The dimensions of the nestbox should be 25 by 25 by 30 centimetres, with an entry hole 6 centimetres across. The bottom is covered with sawdust and peat. The female lays four to eight white eggs measuring 24 by 19 millimetres and sits on them for 20 days. The male feeds her with care and she rarely leaves the nest. She is not sensitive to being disturbed and rarely flies out during inspection. The young leave the nest when they are 4 weeks old and continue to be fed for another 2 to 3 weeks. A brood comprises more males than females as a rule. When the adult male begins to pursue the offspring, they should be transferred immediately.

The basic diet is sunflower and canary seed, millet, a small ration of hemp seed and niger seed, weed seeds and chickweed leaves.

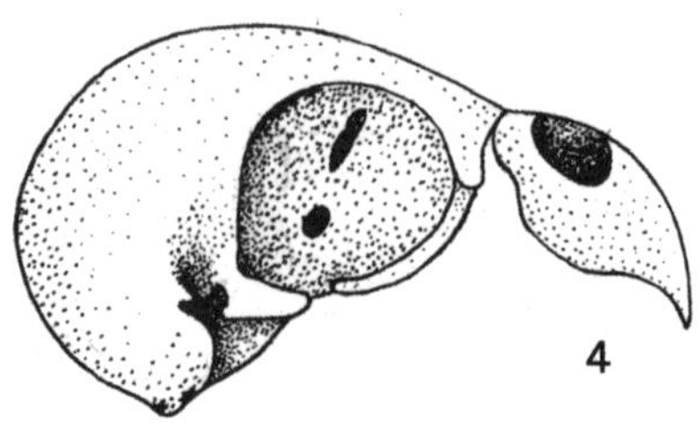

The Red-rumped Parrot reaches a length of 27 to 28 centimetres. The colourful male (1) differs conspicuously from the grey-green female (2). The egg tooth (3) is noticeable in the upper mandible of a one-day-old nestling. The skull (4) shows prominent eye cavities. A pale, pastel-coloured mutation has been bred (5).

The Red-rumped Parrot occurs in two subspecies differing in size and intensity of coloration. It is found in south-eastern Australia, where it is distributed from southern Queensland across New South Wales and Victoria to the eastern parts of

southern Australia. It lives in permanent pairs and the partners mutually preen their plumage, which is a rare phenomenon in Australian parrots. Nests are built in hollow tree trunks and branches, holes in banks of streams, under roofs and in similar places.

Yellow-fronted Parrot Psittacidae

Cyanoramphus auriceps

This is the most popular New Zealand parrot among aviculturists. It is a very affectionate, tame and peaceful bird. It efficiently rears its young, which are easy to tame in captivity and can imitate human speech. The Yellow-fronted Parrot can also be kept singly. It spends most of the time on the ground and does not need many perches. Its strong feet enable it to climb wire netting vertically without using the beak. When foraging on the ground, it uses its feet to dig. The call is reminiscent of a bleating kid, but is more subdued. This parrot is extremely fond of bathing. In spite of its small size, it needs a long cage for flying. It tolerates the European winter.

The Yellow-fronted Parrot is fed sunflower, hemp and canary seeds, oats, wheat, green food, weed seeds, chopped carrots, apples, strawberries, rowanberries and buds of fruit trees. When feeding the young, the birds are served egg mixture as well. Nesting takes place in an artificial box used for Starlings, hung in the sheltered part of the aviary. The clutch of four to nine white eggs is incubated by the female for 19 to 21 days. The young spend some 5 weeks in the nest and are fed mainly by the female which takes the food from the male. Young birds mate when they are only 5 months old. Since Yellow-fronted Parrots spend a great deal of time on the ground, they are susceptible to infection by intestinal parasites, especially ascarids.

The Yellow-fronted Parrot (1) reaches a length of 23 centimetres. The female has a distinctly smaller body and beak than the male and an orange-red iris. Juvenile birds have dark eyes and their foreheads are duller in colour than those of the adults. The occipital bone in the skull is flat (3).

This species is native to New Zealand and the subspecies *C. a. forbesi* lives on Chatham Islands. Another popular species is the Red-fronted Parrot (*C. novaezelandiae*) (2), which occurs in New Zealand and the adjacent islands of Norfolk, New Caledonia, Masquaria and Lord Howe. In the last century, all the species of the genus *Cyanoramphus* were decimated by farmers, and two species are now extinct. These parrots nest in the hollows of dead trees or in rocky crevices.

1 ♂
3

Bourke's Parrot
Neophema bourkii

Psittacidae

Unlike other parrots, Bourke's Parrot does not display a brilliant range of colours, but it is a favourite cage bird because of its good qualities. It is undemanding, quiet, and easy to tame and breed. It has a pleasant, melodious voice. Since it does not damage wood, the aviary can be planted with live greenery. It can also be kept indoors, either singly or in the company of other birds.

Bourke's Parrot is fed canary seed, millet, setaria, a little poppyseed, niger seed, flax seed and small sunflower seeds. The diet is supplemented with chickweed, grated carrots, and in the nesting time the birds should be served hard-boiled eggs, sponge, germinating seeds and unripe grass seeds.

The nestbox should measure 17 by 17 by 25 centimetres, with an entry hole 4.5 centimetres in diameter, and the bottom should be covered with peat and sawdust. The female lays three to six white eggs measuring 20 by 17 millimetres and incubates them for 18 days. The young leave the nest at the age of 4 weeks. They are quite wild at first but soon become tame. Their coloration is the same as in the female, but the plumage is duller. Full coloration is assumed when the young are 7 to 9 months old. There are two broods a year as a rule, and a third one must be prevented for health reasons. Bourke's Parrot can successfully rear parrots of the same genus or even other genera. It is suited for outdoors and in the winter months withstands freezing temperatures down to a minimum of 5 to 7 degrees Centigrade below zero.

2 ♀

The male (1) of this parrot, measuring 19 to 21 centimetres, has a blue band on the front of the head, which is absent in the female (2). Bourke's Parrot was discovered in Australia in 1835, and it was named after the governor of New South Wales, Sir Richard Bourke. It was scientifically described and depicted by John Gould in 1841 and the first brood was reared in captivity in the London Zoological Gardens in 1867.

Bourke's Parrot is a resident of arid steppe regions in central Australia. Its area of distribution is irregular because the bird wanders. It was thought to be extinct, and its numbers increased only recently. Nesting takes place in hollow branches some 3 metres above the ground (3). Food is sought mainly on the ground where the colour of the plumage camouflages the bird. Bourke's Parrot is active chiefly early in the morning and before sunset.

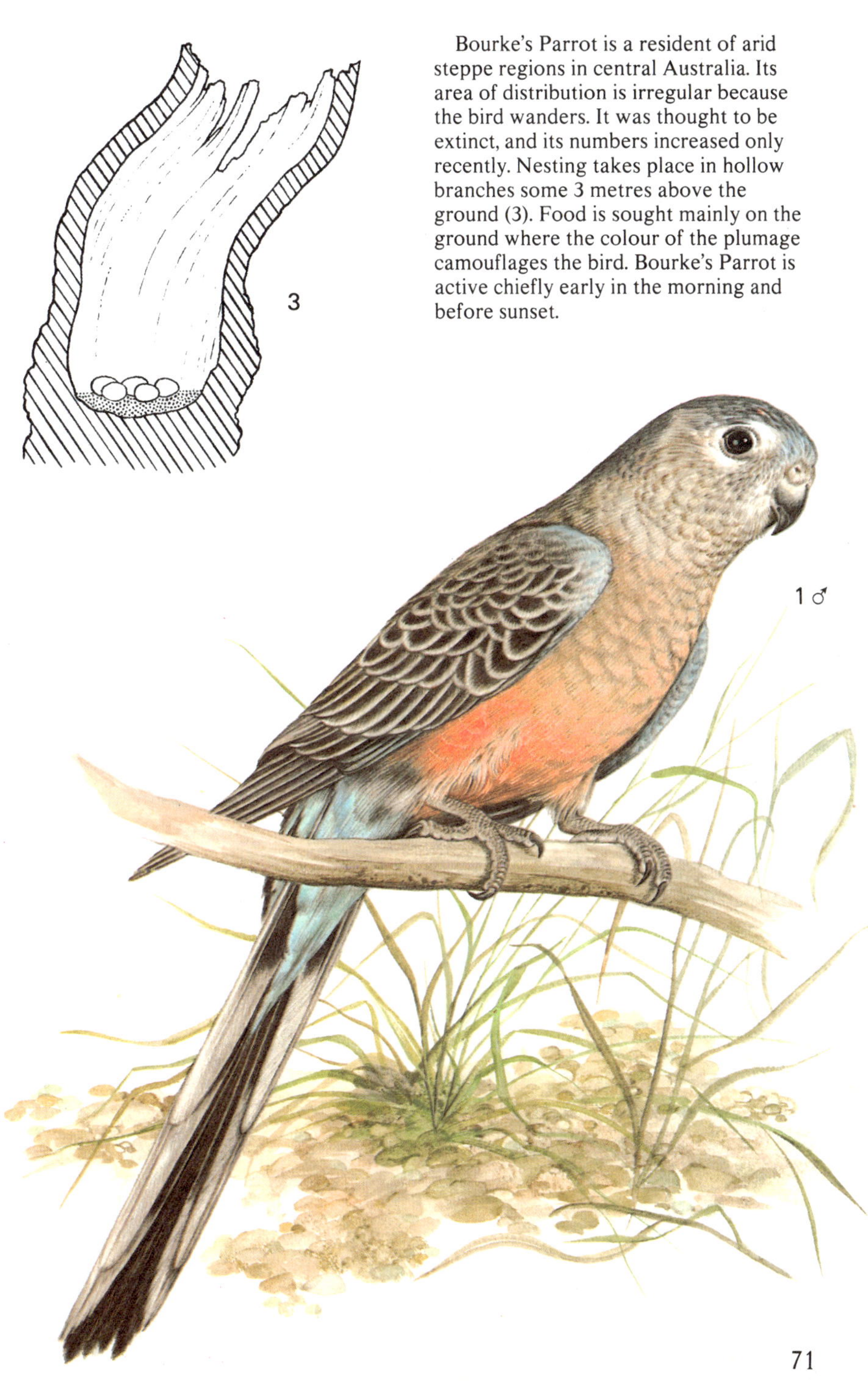

Turquoise Parrot
Neophema pulchella

Psittacidae

At the beginning of the 1960s, the Turquoise Parrot was a rarity in the aviaries of Europe. Now, this prolific bird is widespread and very common. It has a pleasant and melodious voice.

The Turquoise Parrot is kept in a cage, an indoor or outdoor aviary. It withstands the European winter without problems. Birds that are kept singly are easy to tame and become charming companions. For breeding purposes, it is ideal to have an outdoor aviary without heating, about 2 metres long. The construction can be wooden because Turquoise Parrots will not destroy it. They can be given fresh twigs to nibble on.

The birds are served canary seed, millet, niger seed, flax seed, oats and sunflower seed. Important supplements are apples, carrots, chickweed and weed seeds. Germinating setaria and chopped hard-boiled eggs are added in the breeding season.

The Turquoise Parrot is undemanding in nesting requirements, using a rectangular or spherical artificial box suited for Starlings. The female lays four to six white eggs measuring 23 by 18 millimetres on a layer of peat and sawdust. Incubation takes 18 to 20 days and the young leave the nest after 3 weeks to be fed for another 3 weeks by their parents before they are able to fend for themselves. They should be transferred at that time, and the adults will usually start preparing for another clutch. Turquoise Parrots will tolerate nest inspection.

The male (1) of this parrot, about 20 to 21 centimetres long, has a blue head and red patches on the shoulders. The female (2) lacks these patches and the blue colour of the head is duller. An orange-red spot on the abdomen (3) can presently be seen in many Turquoise Parrots. Its origin is unknown; it is not the result of cross-breeding. The female shows a white band (4) on the underside of the wings, while the male's wings are uniform in colour (5).

In the Australian countryside, the Turquoise Parrot is a rare bird and is on the list of protected species. It lives sporadically in southern Queensland, New South Wales and northern Victoria. It frequents thinly covered semi-steppe areas, seeking hollow stumps for nesting. It forages for its food mainly on the ground.

Scarlet-breasted Parrot
Neophema splendida

Psittacidae

Less than twenty years ago, the Scarlet-breasted Parrot was an extremely rare bird among European aviculturists. Many of the parrots, native to deserts, could not tolerate humid weather and perished. Acclimatization was slow but successful and Scarlet-breasted Parrots are now common in captivity.

They are fed on canary seed, millet, setaria, and small sunflower seeds. Good supplements are niger seed, poppyseed, flax seed, lettuce seed and hemp seed. Carrots, apples, chickweed and half-ripe weed seeds must be served regularly.

The Scarlet-breasted Parrot can be kept in a large indoor cage or aviary, although an outdoor aviary with a shelter is best for this parrot. The shelter must be dry and protected from draughts. Heating must be provided in freezing, foggy or humid weather. For nesting, the parrots must be given rectangular or spherical Starling-type nest-boxes. Some females have been observed, both in captivity and the wild, to stick pieces of leaves and grass stalks, up to 3 to 4 centimetres long, into the feathers on the rump and carry the material to the nest in this way. Fresh stalks and leaves maintain a moist environment for the eggs. The clutch numbers three to six white eggs measuring 23 by 19 millimetres. The young hatch within 19 days and the parents feed them for some time after they have fledged. The adult birds do not threaten the young and immediate separation is not necessary.

This species attains a length of 21 centimetres. The male (1) shows a magnificent red patch on the breast; the female lacks this ornament (2). Juvenile birds resemble the female in appearance, but their colours are duller. They assume their full coloration after 3 to 5 months. Blue (3) and yellow (4) varieties have been bred in captivity; these are still extremely rare.

The Scarlet-breasted Parrot is indigenous to Australia, where it is confined to the inland semideserts of the south. It nests in hollow branches of low trees and bushes, and seeks food on the ground, concentrating on grass seeds of the genus *Spinifex*. An inhabitant of arid regions, it does not drink much. Some individuals, however, are fond of bathing in captivity.

Budgerigar
Melopsittacus undulatus

The Budgerigar is the best-known and most frequently kept parrot. It breeds well in captivity. It was scientifically described by G. Shaw in 1805, but it became known through John Gould who brought it to England in 1840. In the following years, the birds were imported in such numbers that their export from Australia had to be prohibited.

The Budgerigar can be tamed and kept freely, even in a flat. It will sit on the owner's hand when called and learn to imitate words. Budgerigars are very hardy and can be left outdoors throughout the year. Breeding is assured by one pair kept in a cage or aviary. When keeping Budgerigars for exhibitions, pairs have to be separated to avoid cross-breeding and to preserve heredity. In a large aviary, there should be sufficient birds to allow them the freedom of choosing their partners. The pairs formed are permanent.

The diet is simple: various sorts of millet, canary seed, both hulled and unhulled oats, chickweed and apples. Budgerigars are undemanding as regards the nestbox. They use boxes placed upright or lengthwise with a base about 20 centimetres square, 25 to 30 centimetres high, having an entry hole with a 6 centimetres diameter. A bowl-shaped nesting cup should be made in the bottom and covered with sawdust. The clutch contains five to six, exceptionally ten, white eggs measuring 19 by 14 millimetres. The female starts sitting after laying the second egg, and the young hatch at one-day intervals after 17 to 18 days. The young are fed for 5 weeks in the nest by both parents. Some 2 weeks after fledging, juvenile Budgerigars should be transferred to another cage.

Budgerigars are widespread throughout Australia except the coastal areas. They are about 19 centimetres long. The specimens seen in the wild are green (1). In long-lasting periods of drought, Budgerigars migrate in large flocks. On arrival at a suitably rainy locality, they start nesting immediately and leave the countryside when the young are fledged. In the drought season, they seek watering-places and tens of thousands of these birds sometimes gather near water.

Juvenile birds have a blue-white area around the nostrils (2) and the beak of a one-day-old nestling shows the egg tooth (3). Many colour mutations have been bred in captivity: the first lutino Budgerigars (4) were bred in 1872, followed by violet (5), grey (6) and other mutations. In the original green male Budgerigars, the colour around the nostrils is blue (7) and in the female it is brown (8). This is not true of some (mainly light-coloured) mutations.

Grey Parrot
Psittacus erithacus

Psittacidae

The Grey Parrot excels all other birds in its ability to imitate human speech. Not only can it mimic words with the owner's accent, it is also able to associate them with things or circumstances; for example, it will say 'good night' and 'good morning' spontaneously at the appropriate times. A well-tamed Grey Parrot completely forgets its natural call.

The diet covers sunflower seed, peanuts and other nuts, sponge, fruit, green food and curds. Some aviculturists recommend lean boiled veal.

Singly kept birds should be housed in a large rectangular cage fitted with china vessels and a well-secured door. Once or twice a week the bird should be sprayed with tepid water or exposed to a summer rain. It also enjoys basking in the morning and evening sun. This species has a long life expectancy of over seventy years. Some individuals never become quite tame although they mimic sounds.

An outdoor aviary is best suited for breeding in captivity. The wire netting on a metal frame should be of thick gauge and the shelter must be heated in winter. The nestbox must have thick walls and dimensions of 35 by 35 by 60 centimetres with an entry hole 12 centimetres across. The female lays two to four eggs at three-day intervals and incubates them for 29 to 30 days. Young Grey Parrots have pale feet and beaks. They leave the nest when they are 10 weeks old.

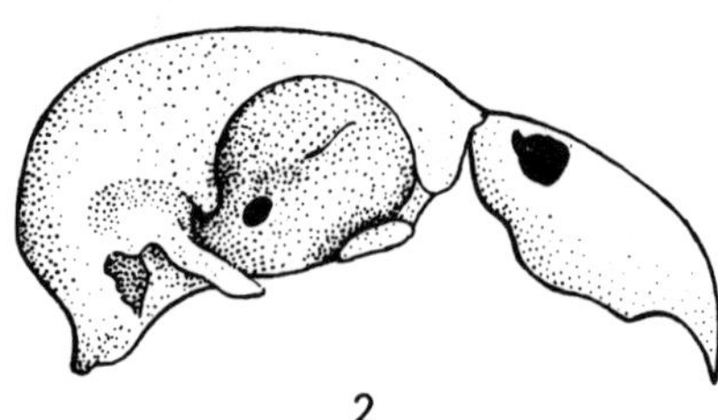

2

The length of the Grey Parrot (1) is 36 centimetres and the sexes are difficult to distinguish. The female usually has a smaller head, beak and body than the male. The skull of the Grey Parrot (2) is angular, with a massive upper mandible and a large, backward-turned outgrowth on the occipital bone.

In Africa the Grey Parrot lives in the western forest areas of Guinea, Sierra Leone, Liberia, Ivory Coast, Congo and Angola. The south is inhabited by the pale grey subspecies *P. e. erithacus,* the rarer dark grey *P. e. timneh* occurs in the north. The subspecies *P. e. princeps* is found on the islands of Principé and Fernando Pó in the Gulf of Guinea. Outside the nesting season, Grey Parrots live in colonies and roost in the tallest trees at night. They set out for long foraging trips every morning, in search of various fruits and seeds.

Senegal Parrot
Poicephalus senegalus

The Senegal Parrot can be kept singly in a cage or in pairs in an indoor or outdoor aviary. The winter temperature should be 10 to 12 degrees Centigrade. When well treated, young birds grow up to be very peaceable, affectionate and tame companions. Only young specimens are recommended for taming, they are distinguished by their dark iris which turns yellow when the birds are a year old.

Solid perches of oak or beech wood should be put in the cage. For nesting purposes, the birds should be placed in an outdoor aviary. The difficulty in distinguishing the sexes is enhanced by differences occurring with age and subspecies. The best guide is usually the behaviour of the parrots. Natural nestboxes are best, although young Senegal Parrots have been bred in artificial boxes. These should measure 25 by 25 by 35 to 60 centimetres, with an entrance hole 7 cm across. The male performs his nuptial dance with wings spread in a fan-like shape, erecting the feathers on the neck and making strange sounds. The female lays three eggs as a rule and incubates them for 22 days. The male stays near the entry hole during this time. The young leave the nest after 11 weeks. Juvenile birds have a dark grey cap and ash-grey cheeks.

The Senegal Parrot is fed sunflower seed, oats, canary seed, a variety of nuts, maize, wheat, apples and carrots. Soft food is not taken by all individuals.

The Senegal Parrot attains a length of 24 centimetres. The female is very similar to the male (1), sometimes having duller plumage. The male has a striking yellow to orange-red abdomen (2). The head of a one-day-old nestling shows a prominent egg tooth and large ear orifices (3).

This species is native to western Africa where it extends from Senegal to Cameroon in three subspecies, the most handsome being *P. s. versteri* with a rich orange-coloured abdomen. This is a plentiful bird in its homeland, causing serious damage to banana and maize plantations. The related species *Poicephalus meyeri* (4) is also often imported and has an attractive coloration.

1 ♂
2 ♂
3

Grey-headed Lovebird Psittacidae
Agapornis cana

This interestingly coloured lovebird displays distinct sexual dimorphism. Breeding succeeds best in an indoor aviary, although some specimens have been bred in a cage or an outdoor aviary. Breeding is often difficult and depends mainly on good pairing. Imported lovebirds show a tendency to nest in autumn. For nesting, they prefer a Budgerigar-type of nestbox which they also use as their sleeping quarters. They may line it very sparsely or cover the bottom with a heap of building material, such as sprays of grass, chickweed, pieces of bark, elder, willow, or with needles, preferably those of larch. The female brings the material stuck in her backside feathers. The clutch is four to five eggs measuring 19.2 by 16 millimetres, which are incubated for 22 days. Young lovebirds leave the nest when they are 5 weeks old and continue to be looked after by the male, while the female gets ready for a second clutch.

Well-acclimatized lovebirds withstand mild frosts. Young birds taken from the nest and reared by man become very tame and affectionate. The call of the Grey-headed Lovebird is 'chilp-chilp'.

The diet is simple: newly imported birds are served canary seed and ears of Senegal millet, while acclimatized birds eat millet, setaria, and green food such as chickweed. When they are feeding their young, they are given germinating seeds, soft food and fruit.

A good quality of the Grey-headed Lovebird, which is 14 centimetres long, is the easy distinction of the sexes. The male (1) has a pale grey head, neck and breast, while the female (2) is green all over. Young imported males are green but those bred in captivity have a grey head when they are fledged.

In the wild, the Grey-headed Lovebird inhabits Madagascar and the adjacent islands in two subspecies. The nominate subspecies *A. c. cana* (1, 2) is slightly smaller than *A. c. ablectanea* (3, 4), which is bluer. For most of the year, Grey-headed Lovebirds live in flocks and frequent the margins of woods and date groves, seeking food in rice paddies.

Peach-faced Lovebird
Agapornis roseicollis

Because of its easy breeding, attractive coloration and affectionate nature, the Peach-faced Lovebird is the most frequently kept species of its genus. It breeds freely in a cage or in indoor or outdoor aviaries. It can spend the winter in an unheated room.

The diet is sunflower or canary seed, millet, oats, apples, chickweed and fruit. Germinating setaria and other seeds are served in the breeding season.

The nestbox should have a base 18 centimetres square and should be 25 centimetres high, with an entry hole 5 centimetres in diameter. The roof should be removable to enable inspection of the nest. Lovebirds must be provided with building material such as pieces of bark, twigs of willow, birch and lime, about 6 to 8 centimetres long, plantain stalks, and so on. The female carries them to the nest stuck in the feathers on her rump, often transporting 5 to 7 such pieces at a time. She builds a solid roofed nest with an entrance at the top; the rear wall of the nesting cup is only lightly covered. The lining has to be made of fresh greenery. The clutch consists of three to five eggs which are incubated by the female for 22 days. The young stay in the nest for 5 to 6 weeks and they are fed by the male for another 2 weeks after they have fledged, while the female is preparing a second clutch. Juvenile birds fly well right after fledging. They must be separated early from their parents who attack them and bite their legs.

The male (1) reaches a length of 15 centimetres. The female is slightly bigger and her head is lighter coloured. Young lovebirds have a blackish-grey beak and their pink-red colour is more subdued. Yellow (2) and pastel blue (3) varieties are also bred.

The Peach-faced Lovebird is indigenous to south-western Africa, where it is resident in arid areas close to deserts, but always near a source of water. Outside the nesting season, it roams the countryside in flocks. Its presence is revealed by a piercing call 'tsik-tsiktsik'. The Peach-faced Lovebird nests in old hollows or occupies the nests of sparrows and weavers.

Fischer's Lovebird

Agapornis fischeri

Psittacidae

The handsomely coloured Fischer's Lovebird is a popular cage and aviary bird. Some experts recommend keeping this species in pairs, although recently they have been successfully bred in small flocks. Thoroughbred birds with clear, sharp-defined patterns should be carefully selected for breeding. The cage has to be at least 80 centimetres long. The Starling-sized nestbox can be hung from the outside. It is advisable to fit an aviary with more nestboxes than there are pairs. The birds must be constantly provided with willow twigs, plantain stalks and so on to build their spherical nest. Fresh greenery maintains moisture around the eggs. The female lays four to eight white eggs measuring 23.3 by 17 millimetres and sits on them for 23 days. The young are fed for 38 days in the nest. After hatching, they have orange-red down, a pale brown beak and flesh-coloured skin and legs. The legs become dark within 12 days and the beak turns red. The second down is a dirty green-grey colour and grows within 16 days. The young are fully fledged within a month. They have a yellow-red beak with a pale reddish tip and until they are 2.5 to 3 months old, there are a few black stripes at the base of their upper mandible.

Adult lovebirds are fed sunflower and canary seed, millet and oats, and they must have fruit, particularly apples, and carrots. Egg mixture is added in the breeding season.

Fischer's Lovebird attains a length of 15 centimetres. The male (1) is almost identical in appearance to the female. According to some experts, the inside vanes of the primaries in the female are pure black, while in the male they are greyer. The outside vanes are broader and greener in the male. The front part of the body in both sexes is outstandingly colourful (2). Consistent breeding has resulted in several colour mutations. The blue mutation with a whitish-grey head and blue wings originated in California.

There is also a yellow mutation (3) whose heredity is recessive (not permanent).

Fischer's Lovebird is native to northern Tanzania, where it lives at heights of up to 1,700 metres. It nests, mostly in colonies, in trees of the genera *Acacia*, *Commiphora* and others, from May to June.

1 ♂

Masked Lovebird Psittacidae
Agapornis personata

This species, which used to breed with difficulty in captivity, has become very popular recently and now breeds more freely. It can be successfully bred even indoors, one pair to a cage. Several pairs can be housed in an outdoor aviary provided the birds are put in at the same time. There should be more nestboxes in the aviary than there are pairs. Masked Lovebirds will nest in a wooden box with a base 15 centimetres square and 25 to 30 centimetres high, with an entry hole 5 centimetres across. The birds must be provided with willow twigs to build their spherical nest. The female brings in the material. The male often scratches his head before mating. The clutch numbers four to six, sometimes eight, eggs measuring 23.3 by 17 millimetres. They are incubated by the female for 21 to 23 days. The female usually starts sitting after laying the third egg, and there is consequently a difference in size between the first and last chick to hatch out. Newly hatched nestlings are covered with orange-red down. The young leave the nest after 44 days and continue to be fed by their parents for another 2 weeks after fledging.

It is advisable to keep Masked Lovebirds at room temperature in winter, although they withstand freezing weather if provided with boxes in which they can sleep.

The diet is the same as for other lovebirds: sunflower seed, millet, oats, setaria, and an abundance of fruit and green food.

Adult Masked Lovebirds reach a length of 15 centimetres. The female and the male (1) are difficult to distinguish. The black colour on the female's head has a brownish sheen, and her head is sometimes slightly bigger than that of the male. Young birds (2) have a browner head and their plumage is a dirty yellow colour. Out of the many colour mutations the blue one (3) is the most attractive.

1 ♂

The Masked Lovebird lives in north-eastern Tanzania and Kenya, in dry grassy steppes with acacias, mimosas and baobabs. The birds move in flocks of twenty to forty and frequent the banks of streams. They nest in hollow branches, but avoid dense and tall forests.

Alexandrine Parakeet
Psittacula eupatria

Psittacidae

The Alexandrine Parakeet has been kept by humans since ancient times, and was a popular bird with patrician Romans. Its size makes it unsuitable for a cage, and it should be placed in an indoor or outdoor aviary which is at least 2 metres long. The aviary is made of metal tubes and strong wire netting, and the sheltered part must also be resistant to the birds' powerful beaks. The diet is sunflower seed, fresh maize, unhulled rice, oats, wheat, a lot of fruit, sponge and green food. When feeding the young, Alexandrine Parakeets are given germinating seeds and egg mixture. They must be supplied with fresh twigs to nibble on.

Since the Alexandrine Parakeet begins to nest in February and March, indoor aviaries are best suited for breeding. In January, the aviary should be provided with a nestbox which is at least 60 centimetres high, with a base 35 centimetres square and an entry hole 9 centimetres across. The female lays two to four eggs measuring 34 by 29 millimetres. She deposits them on a layer of moistened peat and sawdust. In chilly weather, some females have problems laying their eggs, and their health should be checked carefully. The female incubates the clutch for 23 to 24 days, while the male feeds her. The young stay in the nest for about 7 weeks. After fledging, they have the same plumage as the female, only duller in colour. At the age of 18 months, brown spots appear on their shoulders. They mature in their third year.

2 ♀

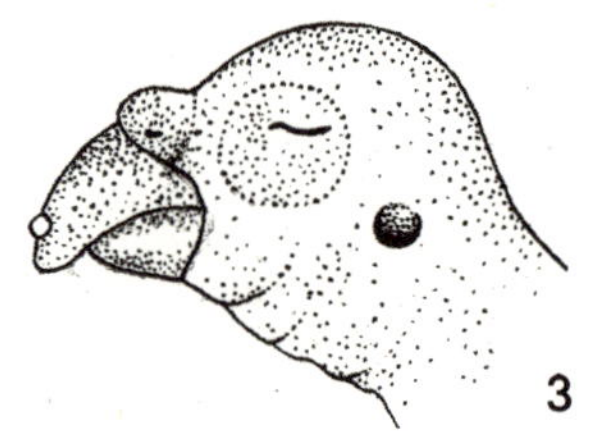

3

The Alexandrine Parakeet reaches a length of 58 centimetres. The male (1) has a ring around its neck, which is pink at the nape and black on the sides and front. The female (2) lacks this ornament. A one-day-old nestling (3) shows a pronounced cere around the beak and an egg tooth. Yellow, blue and white varieties have been bred in captivity.

This parakeet occurs in five subspecies in India, Indochina, eastern Afghanistan, western Pakistan, Sri Lanka and the Andaman Islands. It roams the countryside in large flocks. It is an efficient, fast flier and an adept climber, moving dexterously along branches and rarely descending to the ground. It can be found in hilly and humid mountainous areas covered with dense woods.

Rose-ringed Parakeet
Psittacula krameri

Psittacidae

The Rose-ringed Parakeet is the most commonly kept species of the genus *Psittacula.* It has many advantages: it is frequently imported because of its abundant occurrence in the wild; it has an elegant appearance; it is undemanding and hardy; and it breeds readily. Newly imported birds should be allowed to breed from January to March in an indoor aviary or a large cage. Acclimatized parakeets will breed in spring in an outdoor aviary. The dimensions of the nestbox should be 30 by 30 by 50 centimetres with an entry hole 7 centimetres in diameter. The bottom must be covered with moist peat and sawdust. The courting male flies about the aviary, spreads his tail when he alights to the accompaniment of a melodious jingling phrase, and feeds the female while preening the feathers on her head. The clutch numbers three to five eggs measuring 30.7 by 23.8 millimetres. Incubation is carried out by the female for 22 days. The young leave the nest after 6 weeks and are fed for another 2 weeks or so by their parents. Juvenile birds resemble the female but lack any pattern. They are sexually mature in the third year of life, when they assume their adult coloration.

The Rose-ringed Parakeet is fed sunflower seed, oats, soft maize, wheat, large-grained millet, fruit, carrots, young kohlrabies, green food and fresh twigs. When feeding the young, parakeets are served egg mixture, soaked sponge, germinating grain and a lot of green food.

The Rose-ringed Parakeet cannot be kept along with other species of parakeet, because it is extremely quarrelsome and aggressive.

The Rose-ringed Parakeet grows to a length of about 40 to 42 centimetres. The male (1) has a colourful ring on the neck, which is absent in the female (2). Two mutations have been bred in recent years, blue (3) and lutino (4). Young birds, partly fed by humans before becoming fully fledged, can be easily tamed and taught to mimic sounds and words. One individual was able to repeat some hundred words. The natural call of the Rose-ringed Parakeet is rarely heard in captivity.

This species has the largest area of distribution of all the parakeets. It lives in central and east Africa, Egypt, Mauritius, Zanzibar, Aden, Oman, Kuwait, Iraq, Iran, India, Indochina, south-eastern China and Sri Lanka. Four geographical forms are recognized. The Indian subspecies are imported more often than the African ones.

Plum-headed Parakeet
Psittacula cyanocephala

The plum-headed Parakeet, if kept singly, will soon become tame and affectionate, and learn to imitate words. Pairs of these small parakeets can be kept in a cage, although an indoor or outdoor aviary is preferable. The outdoor construction has to be sheltered and the temperature must be maintained above 0 degrees Centigrade, because all parakeets tend to suffer frostbite on their legs.

If the birds spend the winter in a heated environment, they will start courting between January and April. It is therefore advisable to keep them throughout the winter in an unheated room at a temperature above freezing point, to delay the courtship until the birds can be transferred to an outdoor aviary. The courting male runs along the perch making song-like sounds, suddenly stops and bends forward. The nestbox should have a base about 20 centimetres square and a height of 30 centimetres. The clutch comprises four to six eggs measuring 25 by 20.4 millimetres, and incubation lasts for 22 to 23 days. The young leave the nest when they are almost 6 weeks old and continue to be fed by the male for some time.

The diet is the same as in the Rose-ringed Parakeet, and when the birds are breeding, it is supplemented with germinating oats, soaked and pressed white bread, sponge and egg mixture with green food.

Consistent breeding has resulted in a yellow mutation which has a reddish head, a blue mutation, and a mottled red one.

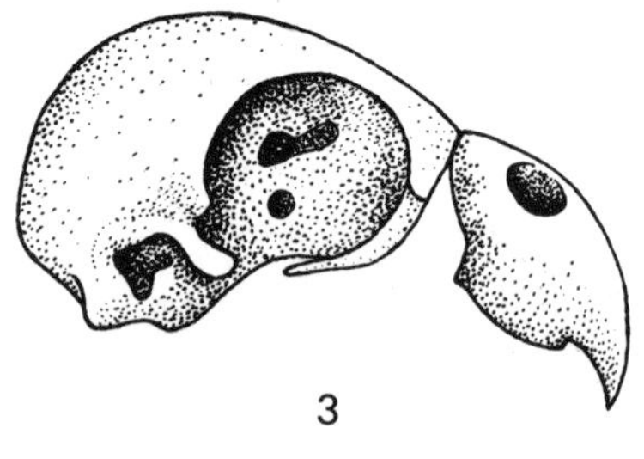

The Plum-headed Parakeet is 33 to 35 centimetres long. The male (1) has a plum-coloured head, while the female (2) has a grey-blue head and lacks the brown spot on the shoulders. Young birds resemble the female, and assume their adult coloration at 2 years of age. The skull of the Plum-headed Parakeet (3) has large eye cavities and protuberances on the occipital bone. This parakeet is a fast flier and its voice is more pleasant than those of other related species.

The Plum-headed Parakeet inhabits the primary forests of Sri Lanka, India, Pakistan, Nepal and Bhutan, occasionally visiting cultivated wooded areas. It forages in small flocks, mainly in trees, rarely descending to the ground. It consumes chiefly fruit and seeds, and raids wheat and maize fields as well as rice paddies.

Blue and Yellow Macaw
Ara ararauna

Psittacidae

Macaws of the genus *Ara* reach the largest size of all the species in the order Psittaciformes. They are valued by bird-keepers for their intelligence, magnificent coloration and tameness. The Blue and Yellow Macaw is the most intelligent and affectionate species in the genus. Young birds are easy to tame and learn to mimic sounds and tunes and reproduce words. Because of these qualities, it is usually kept singly. A newly imported bird is put into a cage. When the owner has got to know its behaviour and character, the bird can be placed on a perch in a room, on which it stays almost all the time.

Breeding is easy, given the mutual affection of the two partners. In spring, macaws are transferred to an outdoor aviary, which does not have to be too spacious but should be made of metal with a thick wire netting and provided with a shelter. The nestbox is either natural or made of wooden planks, with minimal dimensions of 50 by 50 by 80 centimetres and an entry hole 17 centimetres across. The nestbox can be situated on the ground. Two to three eggs, measuring 46.4 by 35.9 millimetres, form the usual clutch. The female sits on them for 24 to 26 days. The young stay in the nest for 13 weeks. When they leave the box, they need a week to learn to fly.

The diet is the same as for all large species of parrots and it has to be varied.

The Blue and Yellow Macaw, with a length of up to 90 centimetres, is a giant among parrots. The male (1) is almost identical in appearance to the female, which is sometimes smaller with a more delicately built head and beak. In an irritated male (2) the bald whitish cheeks turn a sharp pink. This phenomenon is rarely observed in the female, and the intensity of the pink colour is very weak.

2 ♂

3

A young bird (3) resembles the adults but its beak is pale and less hooked, its iris is brown, and the cere and bald cheeks are pink. The skull (4) shows a markedly massive upper mandible and relatively small eye cavities.

It inhabits the primary forests of eastern Panama, southern Colombia, Ecuador, northern Peru, Venezuela, Trinidad, Brazil, Bolivia, Paraguay and northern Argentina. In the wild, it feeds on nuts, berries, buds and young shoots.

Military Macaw
Ara militaris

Psittacidae

The Military Macaw is an affectionate bird which will learn to reproduce a few words, although some experts regard it as less talented a mimic than other species of macaw. A young imported bird becomes tame if treated with care. It may be kept in a room or garden on a perch, which it never leaves. The vessels containing food and water, preferably made of china, have to be thoroughly fastened to the perch, since the bird has an extremely powerful beak. It must be protected from freezing weather in the winter months, as do other related species. The Military Macaw rarely bathes, preferring refreshment in tepid rain, when it tries to soak the feathers on the underside of its wings.

This species is fed sunflower seed, maize, peanuts, wheat, oats, sponge, carrots, apples and other fruit. Twigs for nibbling are a necessary supplement.

The Military Macaw is imported relatively often, and breeding can be attempted in an outdoor aviary. The nestbox has to be as large as for other macaws. The female usually lays two white eggs measuring 46.4 by 32.8 millimetres, which she incubates for 24 to 26 days. The young stay in the nesting cavity for a long time. It is a noisy bird and its 'craa ... aak' can be heard mainly in flight. A young, tamed bird usually stops using its natural voice.

The Military Macaw has been successfully crossbred with other species of its genus.

2

The Military Macaw, which measures up to 70 centimetres, displays no sexual dimorphism (1). There are three subspecies, out of which *A. m. boliviana* (2) has a handsomely coloured head. The Military Macaw is often mistaken for the related species *Ara ambigua* (3), which is a paler green colour with a yellowish shade.

It inhabits both lowlands and mountains in Mexico, Colombia, north-western Venezuela, Ecuador, northern Peru, Bolivia and north-western Argentina. In the Andes, it has been sighted at a height of 3,500 metres. It frequents predominantly the forest canopy, from which it visits maize plantations and fruit orchards. It nests in tree hollows and in Peru its nests have been seen in holes dug out of sandy slopes.

Scarlet Macaw (Red and Yellow Macaw) Psittacidae
Ara macao

This gaily coloured macaw is usually kept singly in large rooms and halls, and transferred to a garden perch for the summer. If well treated, newly imported birds soon become tame and very affectionate. They learn to imitate words but only rarely repeat brief phrases. Young birds often stop sounding their unpleasant and far-carrying 'rraa... aar'. The Scarlet Macaw has a life expectancy of up to 100 years. It is fed a variety of nuts, sunflower seed, maize (mainly fresh), wheat, oats, apples and other fruit, carrots, sponge, and so on. Fresh twigs for nibbling must be supplied.

In spring, a breeding pair is housed in an outdoor aviary covered with thick wire netting. The nestbox must be very roomy; a large wooden barrel can be used. The female lays two to three white eggs measuring 47 by 33.9 millimetres and sits on them for 25 to 27 days. The male guards the entry hole and sometimes visits his mate, but never shares incubation. The young leave the nest after 12 weeks. A single offspring is usually reared, sometimes two but never more.

In the breeding season, the diet is supplemented with boiled rice, green food, hard-boiled eggs, bananas, tangerines, bread and ingredients rich in calcium. Tropical and canned fruit is served in winter. The Scarlet Macaw must spend the winter in a frost-free room.

2 ♀

3

The Scarlet Macaw reaches a length of 85 centimetres. At first sight, the male (1) does not differ from the female. Closer observation reveals a smaller, broader and more hooked beak in the female (2). Young birds (3) have dark eyes and grey lower mandibles. Their small and middle wing coverts are green and the shoulder coverts are green with yellow central parts.

It lives in the rainforests of Central America, Colombia,Trinidad, south-eastern Peru and in the Brazilian provinces of Santa Cruz and Mato Grosso. Its habitat is tall trees where it forages for berries, nuts and shoots. It favours fruits of palm trees and seeds of conifers. In some years, Scarlet Macaws travel to the coast to raid plantations, especially fig trees.

Green-winged Macaw
Ara chloroptera

The Green-winged Macaw is one of the largest species of its genus, attaining a length of 90 centimetres. It is usually kept singly, as this is the best way to tame and teach a newly imported bird. A well-tamed bird can be kept on a perch indoors, and in summer in a garden. It will choose its favourite person — man, woman or child — from among the people who look after it, and will allow this person to handle it, while it may attack the others with its beak. This applies to all other species of macaw as well.

A pair of Green-winged Macaws can be situated in a large outdoor aviary made of strong wire and fitted with a shelter. The birds need a constant supply of fresh twigs to nibble on. For nesting, they should be provided with a large hollow tree trunk or wooden barrel. The female lays two eggs measuring 50 by 35.4 millimetres and sits on them for some 4 weeks. In the incubation period, the relative humidity of the air must be about 85 per cent. To achieve this the layer of sawdust and peat in the nest is moistened and a tray with water is situated underneath the nesting cup. While the nestlings are being reared, the following feeding mixture should be served: a cup of wheat groats, 2 egg yolks and 2 tablespoons of powdered milk are mixed and cooked; one part of bananas and one part of curds are added to six parts of this mixture, together with half-ripe maize, germinating corn and vitamins. The young are fed by both parents. They begin to fend for themselves after some 3 months.

The life expectancy of the Green-winged Macaw is 60 to 80 years. The male (1) and female have the same coloration. His head (2) and beak are bigger than those of the female (3). Young birds (4) have a shorter tail, the lower part of the beak and its upperparts are pale grey at the base, and the iris is brown.

The Green-winged Macaw inhabits the rainforests of eastern Panama, Colombia, Venezuela, Brazil, northern and eastern Bolivia, Paraguay and northern Argentina, ascending to a height of up to 2,000 metres. Macaws move clumsily on the ground. Palm fruits are their favourite food. Nesting takes place high above the ground in hollow trees, and the eggs are laid in spring, before the rainy season. Indians may take the nestlings and tame them.

Chestnut-fronted Macaw
Ara severa

Psittacidae

Imported young birds of this species are easy to tame and can imitate human speech, various tunes and sounds. The quiet voice of the Chestnut-fronted Macaw is a series of 'ka-dak . . . ka-dak . . . keh-ka . . . keh-ka'. The beak is less powerful than in other macaws. This species is very fond of bathing.

For breeding purposes, a pair is situated in an outdoor or indoor aviary provided with a nestbox, preferably natural, measuring at least 30 by 30 by 70 centimetres with an entry hole 10 centimetres in diameter. The bottom of the nestbox should be covered with a thick layer of garden soil mixed with peat to maintain sufficient moisture for the three to five eggs measuring 38.4 by 30.4 millimetres. The young hatch after 24 to 26 days. During incubation the male sits at the entry hole, feeding the female, and sometimes sleeps inside overnight. Juvenile birds are fledged when they are about 2 months old.

In the breeding season, the diet of sunflower seed, unripe or soaked maize, peanuts, germinated wheat or oats, fruit and sponge is supplemented with chopped hard-boiled eggs, sweet rice boiled in milk, sufficient amounts of carrots, apples, green food and germinating seeds. Chestnut-fronted Macaws favour dandelion flowers and nibble on fresh branches.

In a roomy aviary, they can be housed together with other birds, but they become hostile in the nesting period. Well-acclimatized birds can withstand sudden changes in the weather.

2 ♀

3

The male (1) of the Chestnut-fronted Macaw has a pronounced russet band on the forehead; this ornament is narrower and less intensely coloured in the female (2). Juvenile birds (3) have a black iris until the age of 6 months. Young males have a red forehead from their first plumage, while in the females this patch is formed when they are 1 year old.

This species lives in the northern rainforests of South America. Its two subspecies are widely distributed except in Guyana, where its occurrence is rarer. It frequents streams and forages for berries and seeds in the forest canopy. It gathers in flocks outside the nesting season and occasionally visits maize fields and fig plantations.

Red-fronted Conure
Aratinga wagleri

One of the distinctive features of conures of the genus *Aratinga* is their wedge-shaped and graduated tail. These birds are hardy and undemanding in captivity. Young, newly imported specimens which are kept singly can be tamed easily, become affectionate towards their owner and can learn to say a few words. Some tame conures stop sounding their piercing call.

The Red-fronted Conure is best suited to an aviary, where its simple but beautiful coloration can be displayed. It is kept outdoors in summer and indoors in winter. The birds require a temperature above 10 degrees Centigrade. They are highly mobile and destroy wood, so they should be housed in a strong all-wire aviary and supplied with fresh twigs to nibble on.

The diet is sunflower seed, hemp seed, canary seed, millet, peanuts, oats and fruit. When the young are reared, this food should be supplemented with sponge, hard-boiled eggs and more carrots and fruit. The aviary should be fitted with a nestbox, preferably natural, measuring 30 by 30 by 70 centimetres, with an entry hole 8 centimetres in diameter. In Europe the birds usually begin to nest in February. In the courtship period, the two partners turn their heads around and touch each other with their beaks. The female lays two to five large, markedly spherical eggs and incubates them for roughly 28 days. Both adult birds are very aggressive when tending their offspring. When the nest is inspected, the young pretend to be dead. They are green with a yellow beak and leave the nest after 7 weeks.

2

3

The sexes in the Red-fronted Conure (1) are alike in appearance. The modern nomenclature distinguishes four subspecies. *A. w. frontata* (2) is bigger than the nominative subspecies (which is 36 cm long) and the crown coloration reaches the eyes. *A. w. minor* (3) has a rounded rather than angular notch on the upper mandible.

This species lives in the forest zone of northern Venezuela, Colombia, western Ecuador and southern Peru, at heights from 1,000 to 3,000 metres. The birds spend the night in higher situations on hillsides, coming down to valleys to forage. They nest in hollow trees, some 15 to 20 metres above the ground. In western Colombia, their nests have been found in crevices in tall inaccessible rocks.

Yendaya Conure
Aratinga jendaya

Psittacidae

Newly imported specimens of the Yendaya Conure tend to be rather wild and have a penetrating voice. When they are properly treated, they soon become tame. They flourish in an outdoor aviary which should have an iron frame, thick wire netting and a shelter made from stone, brick or other hard material. An all-wire cage can hold only a single tame conure. Acclimatized birds can spend the winter in the unheated aviary. The paired birds stay together and preen each other's plumage. They can be kept with other species of birds.

The Yendaya Conure is fed sunflower seed, millet, oats, a small quantity of hemp seed, maize, nuts, fruit, sponge, boiled rice and green food. When feeding their young the birds are given egg mixture, white bread soaked in milk and germinating seeds. Fresh twigs must be supplied throughout the year.

The birds commence courtship by bowing. The female lays three to five white eggs measuring 28.4 by 22.6 millimetres at 3- to 4-day intervals. Incubation lasts 26 to 30 days and fledging takes 8 weeks. The nestbox should be about 25 by 25 by 30 centimetres, but the birds should be offered several nestboxes of various types and dimensions to choose from. The bottom is covered with moistened sawdust mixed with peat. Some females bring tiny twigs into the nest and bite them into small pieces.

This conure attains a length of 30 centimetres. The male (1) is similar to the female in colour. The female is sometimes less orange below, but as this species is highly variable in colour, this is not a distinguishing feature. Young birds (2) have a pale yellow head and neck, and a pale orange-red abdomen and breast.

This species is relatively abundant in north-eastern Brazil. It lives on berries, seeds, fruit and other plant food. It sometimes causes damage to maize plantations, and it has been seen eating coconuts. For most of the year, Yendaya Conures form family groups or small flocks. They fly fast and straight, forming a beautiful spectacle as their plumage reflects the Sun's rays.

Cactus Conure

Aratinga cactorum

The Cactus Conure was first imported to Europe in 1862 and was bred in captivity in France in 1883. It now breeds freely. It is a peaceable bird and after acclimatization has a long life expectancy. Young birds can be tamed, are affectionate and can learn to reproduce words. The Cactus Conure can be kept in an aviary throughout the year, but temperatures below freezing point must be avoided. Unless it has enough fresh twigs to nibble on, it will damage any wooden parts of the aviary.

Conures seem to be quite demanding in their choice of nest. They usually prefer natural nestboxes to wooden ones, although not always. The box should have a base 30 by 30 centimetres and be 45 centimetres high, with an entry hole 6 centimetres in diameter. The bottom is covered with moistened sawdust. The clutch numbers three to six eggs measuring 25.4 by 19.6 millimetres, which are incubated by the female for some 24 days. The fully feathered young leave the nest at the age of 55 to 60 days. A good pair can rear two broods a year. Some birds can be kept in the company of other species of parrots.

Cactus Conures eat mainly sunflower seed, hulled oats, millet, hemp seed, soaked maize and canary seed. They should get daily rations of carrots, apples or other fruit, willow twigs for nibbling and, occasionally, walnuts. The birds must be given soft egg food with sponge when feeding their young.

The Cactus Conure is about 25 centimetres long. The male (1) differs slightly from the female (2) which has a buff-coloured iris, paler abdomen and greyer head. The juveniles (3) have a greener crown lacking the brown shade, and the throat, breast and abdomen are olive in colour.

It is native to north-eastern Brazil, where it occurs in two subspecies. The nominative subspecies *A. c. cactorum* is found in the south-eastern areas, while *A. c. caixana* lives in the north-east. In its homeland, the Cactus Conure frequents steppe-like regions covered with scrub

and cacti. It nests usually in the hollows of large cacti or in trees. Outside the nesting season, it roams the countryside. It is a shy bird with a piercing voice. Its diet consists of blossoms and fruits of various bushes and cacti, shoots and other plant food.

Peach-fronted Conure
Aratinga aurea

The Peach-fronted Conure, which was first brought to Europe in 1869, is a very popular bird with aviculturists. It is the best-suited species of its genus for keeping: it probably learns more easily, its voice is more pleasant and it does not damage wood so much. It will learn to mimic various sounds such as whistling, sneezing and coughing, and can reproduce words. Imported birds are usually shy and fearful for some time, but they become tame within a few weeks if they are treated correctly.

The diet is sunflower seed, white bread, fruit, canary seed, germinating wheat, maize, sponge, peanuts, some millet, hemp seed and niger.

The Peach-fronted Conure breeds in a cage, even in the company of other parrots, although aviaries, both indoor and outdoor, provide more satisfactory conditions. It is advisable to let the birds choose from more than one nestbox, which should be a hollow tree trunk having minimal dimensions of 20 by 20 by 30 centimetres, with an entry hole 6 centimetres across. It should be lined with moist peat and sawdust. The female lays two to five white eggs measuring 27.4 by 22 millimetres and sits on them for 21 to 26 days. Some males enter the nest but do not share in incubation. Juvenile birds leave the nest when they are 50 days old.

In winter, Peach-fronted Conures should be housed at a minimum temperature of 5 degrees Centigrade. An adequate temperature and humidity should be assured during breeding, which in some pairs begins in March, in others in May. The diet must be varied. These birds always welcome a bath.

This conure attains a length of 26 centimetres. The male (1) differs slightly from the female (2), which has a less elongated patch on the forehead, the feathered area around the eyes is narrower and the abdominal spot is smaller and less bright. Young birds (3) have a grey iris, the orange band on the forehead is narrower and less intense in colour, the crown of the head is a paler shade of blue, and the beak is paler.

The Peach-fronted Conure lives in two subspecies in Brazil, eastern Bolivia, northern Paraguay and north-western Argentina. In the wild, it is a gregarious bird, even in the nesting season. It prefers open country with scrub and woods. It often moves on the ground and it will allow humans to approach it. In addition to seeds and berries, its natural diet contains insects.

Nanday Conure

Nandayus nenday

Psittacidae

The genus *Nandayus* comprises this single, medium-sized (ca 30 cm) species with a long graduated tail. It was imported to Europe in 1870 and was first bred in captivity in France in 1881. Imported birds adapt quickly to their new environment and the lower temperatures. They withstand mild freezing weather when they are sufficiently acclimatized and do not require too much care. However, they suffer frostbite in extreme cold and their legs sometimes break off. A young Nanday Conure, kept singly and tended with great care, can learn to reproduce a few words.

The diet is sunflower seed, hulled oats, hemp seed, millet, canary seed, maize, rice, half-ripe corn and green food. During the feeding of the young, soft food and soaked sponge are served.

The Nanday Conure has a strong, piercing voice, and it is very noisy in the morning and evening and in the courtship period. These conures can be kept, in small flocks or with small songbirds, in an all-wire aviary. They should be provided with fresh twigs to nibble on. The nestbox should be about 20 by 20 by 35 centimetres, with an entry hole 8 centimetres in diameter. The bottom is covered with sawdust or peat. The female lays five to six eggs, one egg every other day, and incubates them for 25 days. She will usually tolerate inspection of the nest. The young gain sight after 23 days, grow their first feathers after 40 to 42 days and they are fully feathered within 50 days. They sometimes leave the nest after 2 months but continue to return there for the night. Nanday Conures like to bathe together.

The magnificent coloration of this species shows best in flight (2). The sexual dimorphism is not distinct. A young bird (3) resembles an adult (1) but its throat and upper breast are less bluish, the tail is shorter and the tarsi are black.

The Nanday Conure lives in the forest areas of south-eastern Bolivia, Mato Grosso in Brazil, Paraguay and northern Argentina. It is a common but heavily pursued bird because its flocks raid fields and orchards. Nanday Conures usually nest in small colonies in tree hollows or in solitary trees in steppes. They move clumsily on the ground and prefer to climb branches of various trees and bushes.

Monk Parakeet

Psittacidae

Myiopsitta monachus

The Monk Parakeet is the only species of parakeet that builds a nest of twigs. A medium-sized bird about 29 centimetres long, it has a graduated tail and a strong beak, and belongs to the monotypical genus *Myiopsitta.* As they are very noisy, these parakeets are not suitable for keeping indoors, but several pairs can be housed in an outdoor aviary. This should provide ample space and be made of a strong frame covered with thick wire netting. The back and the sides should protect the birds from wind and draught. Monk Parakeets can be left outdoors throughout the year, even in harsh freezing weather. Shelves with raised borders are placed in the upper part of the aviary below the roof, on which the nest can be built. In March, a sufficient quantity of branches of willow, hazelnut and other trees, about 20 to 60 centimetres long and 8 to 10 millimetres thick, should be left on the ground. The base of the nest is built by both partners, and the outer part is finished by the male, while the female makes the lining from twigs bitten into small pieces and from grass. The construction takes up to 3 months. The female lays a white egg every other day until the clutch numbers four to six eggs. Duration of incubation is difficult to determine because inspection of the nest is complicated, but it lasts about 22 to 26 days. Young birds stay in the nest for 6 weeks and after fledging begin to seek their own food within a week. Monk Parakeets may rear two broods in a year and will use the same nest for several years. They will return to the aviary if allowed to fly outside. The diet is the same as in most species of parrot.

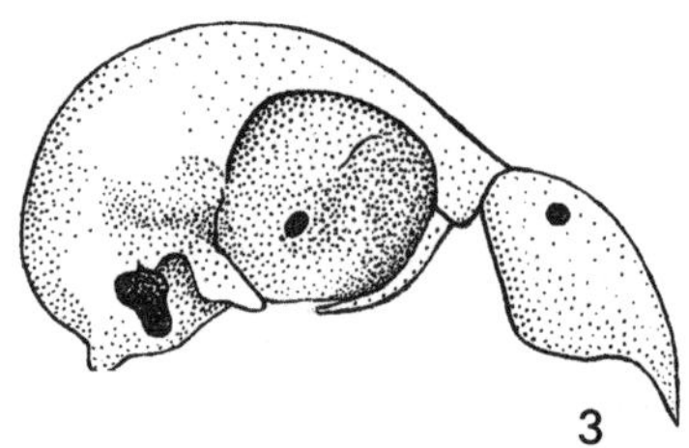

There is no sexual dimorphism in the Monk Parakeet (1). The skull is rounded, with large eye cavities (3).

It is distributed in four subspecies in the humid forest areas of central Bolivia, southern Brazil, central Argentina and Uruguay, occurring at heights of up to 1,000 metres. In the wild, it builds a nest of twigs and sticks in a tall bush or on the outer branches of trees (2). The nest contains a nesting chamber, antechamber and entrance. Thorny twigs of the talaba tree are the most usual building material. The Monk Parakeet is a colonial nester.

First one pair builds its nest and then the others build theirs around it, resulting in constructions up to 3 metres across and weighing over 200 kilograms. Each pair has its individual entrance on the side or at the bottom.

Green-rumped Parrotlet

Psittacidae

Forpus passerinus

The genus *Forpus* comprises small, stout parrots with a massive, laterally flattened beak. The Green-rumped Parrotlet is the most frequently kept species in the genus. Imported birds are shy and acclimatize with difficulty. They should be kept initially at room temperature. Some of the birds, however, have been bred in Europe for many generations and these specimens are quite hardy and can spend the winter months in an unheated room. They tolerate the company of other birds and can be housed in an aviary or birds' room with finch-type songbirds.

Green-rumped Parrotlets feed on canary seed, setaria, hulled oats, small sunflower seeds, various sorts of millet, apples, carrots, soaked figs, chickweed, sorrel and dandelion blossoms. Egg mixture, sponge and germinating, unripe oats should be added to their diet during the breeding period.

They can be kept in a cage at least 50 centimetres long. The nest-box, which should be the same size as for Budgerigars, can be hung either inside or outside the cage. The bottom is covered with peat or sawdust. The clutch numbers three to six eggs. The female lays an egg every 35 to 48 hours and then incubates the clutch for 19 to 21 days. The male feeds her on the nest during this time. The young leave the nest after 5 weeks and the parents feed them for another 2 to 3 weeks. Some fledglings return to the nest for a few nights. In summer, Green-rumped Parrotlets can be kept in an outdoor aviary, where they will breed more freely.

The Green-rumped Parrotlet is only 12 centimetres long. The male (1) differs from the female (2) in the wing colours.

It lives in Trinidad, Guyana, northern and central Venezuela, northern Colombia, northern Brazil, eastern Amazonian region and on the islands of Curaçao, Antilles, Jamaica, Barbados and Martinique. Within this large area, it occurs in five subspecies. Its habitat ranges from dry scrub-covered plains to woods along rivers and dense rainforests. The related species *F. cyanopygius* (3) from north-western Mexico has a blue rump; *F. xanthopterygius* (4) has a dark blue mantle; *F. xanthops* (5) has a yellow head; and *F. coelestis* (6) has a green head and lives in the Pacific area of the Andes, in western Ecuador and in north-western Peru.

Tucuman Amazon
Amazona tucumana

Psittacidae

The Tucuman Amazon is a simply but elegantly coloured parrot. It is usually kept singly, when it can be easily tamed and taught to 'talk'. Its voice, however, always has a 'parrot-like' accent; no Amazon parrot ever forgets its natural piercing call. A well-tamed bird is affectionate and never behaves viciously, being, on the contrary, grateful for any entertainment provided by humans.

The cage has to be 50 to 70 centimetres high, made of wire, with a solid door and solid unbreakable vessels. Rounded cages, painted white, are unsuitable. The Tucuman Amazon can also be kept on a wooden perch about 60 centimetres long. The perch must be fitted to the stand in such a way that it can be replaced when the bird destroys it. Feeding vessels are affixed to the end of the perch so that the bird cannot knock them over and a box filled with sand is situated underneath the stand to collect droppings and remains of food. Climbing on the stand is a useful exercise. The bird must get used to the stand gradually and under supervision, being transferred to the cage at night. It can be left outdoors in summer, where it enjoys occasional tepid rain.

After acclimatization, Tucuman Amazons can spend winter at a temperature of 10 degrees Centigrade. A pair may breed in a large nestbox made of a tree trunk, with an entry hole 15 centimetres in diameter. The clutch usually comprises two to four eggs. Feeding is the same as in other Amazon parrots.

The male (1) is the same colour as the female. Juvenile birds resemble the adults but the plumage on their legs is green (2).

The Tucuman Amazon, about 31 cm long bird, is a typical inhabitant of alder

woods along the eastern foothills of the Andes in south-eastern Bolivia and northern Argentina. It only occurs in north-eastern Argentina outside the nesting season. Tucuman Amazons are abundant in the wild and they can be seen in flocks flying above the forests or seeking food in the treetops. They are denizens of impenetrable tropical rainforests at heights from 1,800 to 2,000 metres. They eat seeds, nuts, berries, blossoms and young shoots. In their homeland they breed in December and January.

Yellow-shouldered Amazon
Amazona barbadensis

Psittacidae

The Yellow-shouldered Amazon has been imported to Europe for many years. It is sometimes sold under other, incorrect names, such as the Yellow-fronted, Yellow-winged and Small Yellow-headed Amazon. Most experts recommend keeping this species singly in order to tame it quickly. It becomes affectionate and learns to 'talk' and imitate the sounds it hears. Each individual has a different talking capacity and even older birds are easy to tame. A very tame bird usually stops using its natural voice. The Yellow-shouldered Amazon can be situated in a cage or on a perch, and may be kept throughout summer in the garden.

The diet is sunflower seed, soaked maize, oats, wheat, a small quantity of hemp seed, carrots, fruit, walnuts and other nuts, figs, berries and green food. Good supplements in the breeding period are sponge and hard-boiled eggs. Fresh young twigs and buds are always appreciated.

For nesting purposes, a pair should be situated in an indoor or outdoor aviary. The nestbox must be large, preferably from a hollow tree trunk. The clutch is usually two to four white eggs measuring 36.7 by 26.1 millimetres. The young stay in the nest for almost 2 months.

The Yellow-shouldered Amazon is 33 centimetres long. The female (2) has a duller coloration than the male (1), and her throat, abdomen and breast are greenish-blue. Juvenile birds (3) resemble the adults, but the underparts lack the blue sheen and the iris is darker and duller.

It occurs in two subspecies which inhabit northern Venezuela and the adjacent islands. The subspecies *A. b. barbadensis* is a continental resident, while *A. b. rothschildi* (4) is found on the island of Bonaire in the Netherlands Antilles and on the islands of Blanquilla and Margarita off the Venezuelan coast. It frequents sparsely wooded and rocky areas near the coast. The birds nest in hollow trees and probably also in rock crevices.

1 ♂
3
4

Blue-fronted Amazon
Amazona aestiva

Psittacidae

This bird was described by Carl von Linné (Linnaeus) in 1758. It is the most frequently imported species of the genus *Amazona.* Its acclimatization is quick and easy, and young birds soon become tame and fond of their owner. They learn to imitate many words and will perform amusing tricks. They can live to be one hundred years old. Single birds are kept in an all-wire cage and must be allowed to take a flight around the room every day.

They are fed sunflower seed, maize, oats, a little hemp seed and millet, wheat, fruit, carrots, and occasionally white bread, sponge and nuts. Despite their hardiness, they should be kept at a temperature of about 12 degrees Centigrade in the winter months.

For breeding purposes, a pair is placed in a medium-sized aviary made of strong material and covered in thick-gauge wire. If it is situated in the garden, the aviary must contain a shelter. The best nestbox is a natural hollow tree trunk, although Blue-fronted Amazons also breed in wooden nestboxes measuring 100 by 40 by 50 centimetres, placed lengthwise. The cavity is filled with wood pulp. The courting male bends forward, knocks at branches with his beak and approaches the female to hand her a twig or leaf and to feed her. This is repeated several times before mating. The clutch is usually composed of two to four eggs which are incubated by the female alone for 29 to 30 days. The young are fledged after roughly 2 months. During the feeding of the young, the diet must be supplemented with hard-boiled eggs, soft food, sponge and tomatoes.

The Blue-fronted Amazon reaches a length of 37 centimetres. The male (1) differs only slightly in colour from the female (2). She is usually smaller, with a smaller head and beak, and the bend of her wing is red, lacking the yellow feathers. There are two subspecies; *A. a. xanthopteryx* differs from the nominate subspecies in the coloration of the wing (3).

It is the most widespread species of its genus, occurring in north-eastern Brazil, Paraguay and northern Argentina. Before nesting in the wild Blue-fronted Amazons gather in certain localities in the rainforest, where they perform their nuptial displays. Flocks of up to 1,000 birds destroy all greenery during their mating rituals, and then scatter to the surrounding countryside to rear their broods.

Hummingbirds Trochilidae

Hummingbirds were first brought to Europe at the beginning of this century. All the imported birds soon perished, the hardiest individual surviving for 9 weeks. New findings in the biology and ethology of hummingbirds, as well as more efficient transportation, resulted in successful breeding in captivity. Today, due to speedy air transport, the American hummingbirds reach Europe in relatively good condition. However, they are demanding and, therefore, are recommended only for specialized aviculturists. Hummingbirds thrive best in glasshouses or in large glass cages planted with greenery and fitted with a thermostat, water-spraying device and heating bulb, where they can enjoy the optimal living conditions throughout the year.

Hummingbirds have to be given substitutes for their natural food, which is nectar from flowers and tiny flying insects. During the day, a large test-tube fitted with a small sucking tube is situated in the cage. It contains a protein solution composed of 1½ teaspoon of Mellin's Baby Formula, 1½ teaspoon of Ledinac meat extract, 3 teaspoons of powdered milk, 8 drops of Vipenta vitamins and 0.12 l of sugar all mixed with water to obtain 0.5 litre (the concentration of sugar solution should be 24 per cent). About 25 Drosophila per bird are served daily. This food is removed in the evening and replaced with a solution of 3 parts water, 1 part sugar and 1.2 parts honey. It remains in the test-tube until the morning because it does not spoil and the birds drink it before their regular daily feed.

In recent years, hummingbirds have been successfully bred in captivity. The female lays two white eggs which she incubates for 12 to 16 days. The young stay in the nest for 14 days and the female feeds them on nectar.

Hummingbirds are native to the tropical, subtropical and temperate zones of South and North America. They occur mainly in lowlands, although some species ascend to a height of 5,000 metres. They live either singly or in pairs and display extreme hostility towards all other birds, including their own species. The males fiercely attack one another in flight.

The large family Trochilidae comprises some 320 species of hummingbirds. Their size, shape and coloration are so rich and variable that no other group of birds can compete with them.

The Sparkling Violet-ear (*Colibri coruscans*) (1) has been popular with aviculturists for some years. The species *Topaza pella* (2) from the north-east of South America has crossed tail feathers, while *Sappho sparganura* (3) from Bolivia, Argentina and Peru has a forked tail. The bright colours of hummingbirds can be seen in the heads of the following species: *Lophornis adorabilis* (4), *Chalcostigma herrani* (5), *Colibri serrirostris* (6) and *Calypte anna* (7).

Toucans

The family Ramphastidae comprises some sixty species of very interesting birds with massive beaks, which are often brightly coloured. The robust beak is, in fact, extremely light and does not represent any burden for the bird. The tongue is long and narrow, the edges being covered with forward-pointing fibres. When sleeping, toucans assume an unusual position with their tail feathers erect and the beak placed on the back between the wings.

In captivity, toucans are very undemanding and hardy, but they have to be sheltered from frost in winter. They can be easily tamed and are as intelligent as parrots. Because of their size and mobility, they have to be kept in indoor glass aviaries. In summer, they can be transferred to the garden. Smaller birds must never be put into the same aviary, since the toucans will kill and devour them. Their excrements are liquid and the bottom of the aviary should, therefore, be covered with peat.

Toucans are fed fruit, boiled rice, soaked white bread, and raw or boiled meat, ground or cut into small pieces. Good supplements are large insects, sparrows and white mice. Some species throw the food up in the air and catch it in the half-open beak.

These birds nest in large hollow trunks and both parents share in incubating one to four pure white eggs. The young hatch after 16 to 18 days, grow slowly and leave the nest after 6 weeks.

Toucans are restricted to the forests of tropical Central and South America. Some species occur at a height of 3,500 metres. They are good fliers but usually cover only short distances. The aborigines often take young toucans and tame them. The first and fourth toes of a toucan's foot are turned backwards (4). A cross-section of the beak shows a fine-boned structure filled with air chambers (5) making the beak solid, resilient and light.

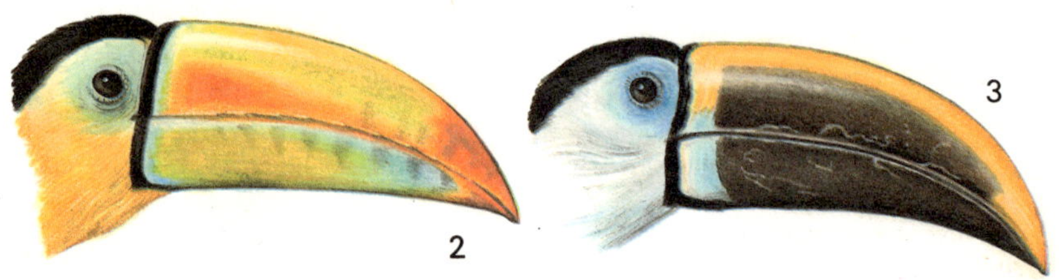

The Toco Toucan (*Ramphastos toco*) (1) is one of the largest species of its genus, reaching a length of 56 to 60 centimetres. It lives in South America, ranging from Guyana across Brazil, Bolivia and Paraguay to northern Argentina. Attractively coloured beaks can be seen in the species *R. sulphurata* (2) and *R. cuvieri* (3).

Pekin Robin

Leiothrix lutea

Timaliidae

The Pekin Robin is one of the few birds possessing all the qualities prized by aviculturists: it is handsomely coloured, an excellent songster, breeds freely in captivity, and it is hardy and tame. It was first brought to Europe in 1866, to the London Zoological Gardens.

Lovers of songbirds keep the males of this species singly in cages. The song is melodious, loud and reminiscent of the call of the European Blackcap (*Sylvia atricapilla*). However, the bird can become so noisy that the cage has to be transferred to the garden or balcony.

The diet is a soft mixture of grated carrots, hard-boiled eggs, breadcrumbs and hard curds, to which are added daily a few mealworm larvae and pieces of fruit. This diet is supplemented from time to time with crushed hemp seed, rape and canary seed, hulled oats and a small quantity of poppyseed, flax seed and niger. The seeds are only supplements, not the basic diet. Insects are added in the breeding season.

Breeding succeeds best in an outdoor aviary densely overgrown with shrubs, containing sufficient insects for the birds. In this environment, Pekin Robins usually hide in the thickest cover and build a tidy, open nest in the highest branches of a shrub. In Europe, they nest in spring and summer. The clutch of three to five eggs is incubated by both parents, and the young hatch after 12 days. They are fledged after 3 weeks. Pekin Robins can spend the winter in a covered outdoor aviary.

2 ♀

The adult bird is 15 centimetres long. The male (1) is almost identical to the female but she lacks the golden sheen on the crown of her head (2). The eggs (3) are bluish-green with russet spots. Young birds are predominantly ash-grey, assuming adult coloration after 12 to 14 weeks.

The Pekin Robin is found in several subspecies in the dense forest areas of northern India, northern Burma, southern China and northern Indochina. In the wild, this bird is extremely active, constantly seeking insects in the bushes. In the courting period, the males mark their nesting territories by loud singing. In the Himalayas, the local inhabitants keep Pekin Robins as cage birds.

Superb Tanager
Calospiza fastuosa

Thraupidae

The large group of tanagers comprises birds of different sizes and coloration, but all have nine primaries, twelve tail feathers, and sometimes almost invisible notches on the tip of the upper mandible. The Superb Tanager is the most frequently kept species in this genus, being a gem of any indoor and outdoor aviary. It is a very quiet bird, tolerant even of smaller species of birds.

The diet is fruit, elderberries, grapes, honey, soaked sponge, custard, maize flour porridge, and sweetened milk or cream. In winter, Superb Tanagers are served soaked dried figs, dates, raisins, and all the available exotic fruit. This food is supplemented daily with egg mixture and a few live insects. Mealworm larvae and bananas are served in small quantities to prevent the birds from getting fat. For the same reason, if they are kept in a cage it should be fitted with only a few perches, so that the birds are forced to fly around. However, Superb Tanagers are not really suited for cages, because as fruit-eaters they take large quantities of food rich in liquid and have fast digestion, and, therefore, soil the bottom considerably. This should be covered with several layers of paper, replaced every day. Tanagers flourish in an aviary planted with shrubs, where they can catch flies, spiders, and so on. They usually nest in an open nestbox concealed in the greenery. The recommended winter temperature is 15 degrees Centigrade.

The Superb Tanager reaches 14 centimetres in length, its wing measuring 7 centimetres, and the tail 5 centimetres. The male (1) differs from the female only in the colour of the head, the female's head (2) being bluer and less shiny. The plumage of the Superb Tanager gleams in the sunshine.

This species is native to eastern Brazil. In the wild, it builds its nest in thickets. The nest is cup-shaped and made of plant material. The clutch numbers two to four eggs which are incubated for 15 days. The young are fed predominantly on insects. They start growing feathers within a week and leave the nest when they are 3 weeks old. Adult birds eat soft berries and fruits, insects, and so on.

1 ♂

Yellow-winged Sugar Bird
Cyanerpes cyaneus

Coerebidae

An aviculturist admiring the beauty of hummingbirds but not daring to keep them because of their food requirements can find the same attractive features in the less-demanding Yellow-winged Sugar Birds. They are served daily a fresh nourishing solution in small glass containers or automatic feeding vessels, so as not to soil their feathers with the sticky liquid. The solution consists of one part condensed milk, one part honey and ten parts water. A supplement of one part meat extract, one part dried eggs and one part biscuit flour can be added. Sugar Birds must be given soft fruit, which in winter is replaced by canned fruit. This diet is supplemented with insects such as small mealworm larvae, *Daphnia,* mosquito larvae, *Drosophila,* fresh ant cocoons, and so on. With suitable feeding, they can live to be 15 years old in captivity.

The perches in the cage should be of natural twigs which are frequently changed. The bottom of the cage is covered daily with blotting paper. These birds thrive best, however, if placed in an indoor aviary or a small summer glasshouse with live plants, where they can nest. A container of water for bathing is essential.

This species has developed a strong sexual dimorphism. The male (1) has black-blue nuptial plumage, while the female (2) is green, darker above and paler below. Outside the courting season, the male resembles the female but has red legs (3). When disturbed, he erects the feathers on the head in a semi-crest (4). The Yellow-winged Sugar Bird reaches a length of 12 centimetres. The spring moult begins in January, the autumn moult occurring in September. A courting male sounds a melodious nuptial call reminiscent of the song of the European Willow Warbler (*Phylloscopus trochilus*).

The home of this bird is Central America, Cuba and the northern part of South America. It occurs as far south as southern Brazil and northern Argentina.

Red-crested Cardinal

Fringillidae

Paroaria coronata

This beautifully coloured bird is kept for both its attractive appearance and song. It was first brought to Europe in 1783 and exhibited in the London Zoological Gardens. The first successful breeding in captivity took place in Florence in 1837. If it is wanted as a songbird, the male is kept singly. If kept in a cage or aviary with other species of birds, the Red-crested Cardinal will tolerate some species and attack others.

Its diet is millet, oats, canary seed, wheat, unhulled rice, sunflower seed, maize, rape, and so on. Green food, fruit and seasonal buds of trees and bushes are added. An egg mixture is served every other day. Fresh water has to be available all the time, because Red-crested Cardinals are fond of bathing. They are very hardy and can spend winter in an enclosed outdoor aviary. When well treated, they live for up to 20 years.

For breeding purposes, the birds should be housed in a large outdoor aviary planted with bushes, where they build a nest or settle in an open nestbox. Nesting is preceded by courtship during which the male dances around the female with a stalk in his beak, with wings hung down and tail feathers spread. The clutch consists of three to six eggs which are usually incubated by the female alone for 15 days, although, in some pairs, the birds take turns. During incubation, the diet of the adult birds is supplemented with unripe millet, ears of corn and various insects. Juvenile birds leave the nest after 17 days, and the parents feed them for another 3 weeks.

The Red-crested Cardinal reaches a length of 18.5 centimetres, the wing measuring 9.5 centimetres and the tail 7 to 8 centimetres. The female is like the male (1) in appearance. The male's crest is usually folded (2); he erects it only when disturbed. Young birds (3) have

a brown head without the crest, and the upperparts are brownish. They grow the crest within 7 weeks of hatching, but they do not assume the adult plumage until their second year.

This species lives in South America, ranging from southern Brazil and Bolivia southwards to central Argentina.

Virginian Cardinal
Pyrrhuloxia cardinalis

Fringillidae

This is probably the most beautiful species of cardinal. It was imported to Europe in the eighteenth century and soon began to breed in captivity. It became very popular due to its hardiness. When in daily contact with humans it becomes very tame, especially young individuals. It is kept singly for its pleasant but loud song, or in pairs which breed relatively well in indoor or outdoor aviaries. If it is provided with thick greenery, it builds a simple nest lined with fine grass. It also nests in wooden boxes with a base 15 centimetres square and 7 centimetres high, or in special cages for singing Canaries. The female lays two to five eggs, which are usually bluish-green with dark brown spots. The clutch is incubated by both partners during the day and by the female alone at night. The young hatch after 12 to 14 days and leave the nest after 16 days, although they are not able to fend for themselves until they are 5 weeks old.

Virginian Cardinals are fed millet, canary seed, oats, buckwheat, rape and sunflower seed, fruit, chickweed and green food. Buds of trees and bushes are welcome in winter. When the young are being fed, egg mixture with curds and ant cocoons are added, as well as mealworm larvae and insects collected by sweeping (avoid contamination by chemical spray). The birds need plenty of fresh water for drinking and bathing. They can be left outdoors throughout the winter months, provided the aviary is well sheltered on all sides.

The male (1) is red and the female (2) is pale brown. Juvenile birds resemble the adults but lack the black pattern on the head, and the beak is black-brown. After the first moult, their coloration is like that of their parents except for the beak, which becomes red when they are 3 years old. The drawings (3) show the male alighting on a branch, as he assumes an erect posture by inertia from the flight.

The Virginian Cardinal is found in the south-eastern and southern United States and in Mexico. Its average length is 19 to 22 centimetres. It seeks low thickets, mainly along water courses, but it also occurs in thin woodland, parks and gardens. It forms pairs in the nesting season, roaming the countryside in small groups at other times.

3
1 ♂

Nonpareil Bunting
Passerina ciris

Fringillidae

The Nonpareil Bunting is a hardy bird but it must be kept in a frost-free environment. The female is more delicate than the male. The magnificent colours of this bird, particularly the red, tend to fade in captivity, which is probably due to the diet. The male, however, remains attractive for many years. Some individuals survive in captivity for as long as sixteen years.

The diet is millet, canary seed, niger, lettuce and flax seed, a little poppyseed, orach and alder. Whenever available, chickweed and lettuce should be served in large amounts, and, occasionally, ant cocoons and mealworm larvae. Some aviculturists give their birds fruit such as bananas or oranges cut crosswise. In the breeding period, the birds need a variety of insects.

The males, which are often kept singly in cages, sing their monotonous but pleasant song all year round. Nonpareil Buntings nest readily in an aviary overgrown with bushes and grass. Breeding is also successful in an indoor glass cage with potted plants. The birds build an open nest woven from dry grass, fine roots, hair, and so on, but they nest readily even in a small box or a nestbox for Canaries. The female lays three to five eggs, incubates them for 13 days, and the young leave the nest 11 days after hatching.

The size of this bunting is 12.5 to 14 centimetres. The colourful male (1) differs markedly from the yellow-green female (2). From the front (3), the male displays his bright red underparts. The eggs are bluish and red-spotted (4).

The Nonpareil Bunting occurs in the southern regions of the United States, Mexico and in all Central American countries. It also lives in the Bahamas and Cuba. The birds from the northerly regions winter in Central America. They often visit fruit plantations in the vicinity of human settlements. In the wild, they build their nests in low thick bushes, and in garden hedges. They sound their call in flight and late in the evenings.

Indigo Bunting
Passerina cyanea

Fringillidae

The Indigo Bunting is suitable for keeping in a cage or aviary. It is a quiet and undemanding bird which, after thorough acclimatization, can withstand temperatures around 2 degrees Centigrade below zero. At lower temperatures the more delicate females ruffle their feathers to keep warm, but the males tolerate 12 degrees Centigrade below zero. This species can be fed canary seed, millet, niger, lettuce and flax seed, poppyseed, orach, alder, green food, egg mixture and a large quantity of insects. Mealworm larvae, fresh ant cocoons and insects caught by sweeping in the grass are also served. Some individuals refuse to eat green food and germinating millet.

In an aviary planted with bushes, the birds readily build a nest and the female lays two to five eggs. Indigo Buntings also nest in an open nestbox or in a special box for canaries, situated outside a cage. If the adult birds' diet after the hatching of the young is composed only of seeds, green food and egg mixture, ant cocoons and mealworm larvae, the offspring will not survive; the parents will throw the 12-day-old chicks out of the nest. If the birds are given a great quantity of insects, spiders, grasshoppers and so on, they usually rear a single young. Failures in breeding are probably caused by lack of variety in the diet at the time when the young are fed. Crossbreeding with Canaries has produced rare hybrids, but has failed to create blue Canaries.

The Indigo Bunting is 12.5 centimetres long. The male in its nuptial plumage (1) is dark blue, with a lighter coloured front part to the body (3). The nuptial plumage is assumed in spring and in the autumn the male moults back into its ordinary plumage of rust-brown upperparts, buff underparts and off-white throat and

2 ♀

1 ♂

abdomen (4). The female (2) has brownish upperparts, a paler head and back, and whitish underparts. In winter, the female has pale brown edges to the large wing coverts.

This species occurs in the eastern United States, Mexico and Central America as far south as Panama. It builds its nest low down in thickets.

Canary
Serinus canaria

Fringillidae

The Canary was kept by Spaniards in the Middle Ages, mainly in monasteries. From Spain, the birds were brought to Italy, and the first Italian Canaries appeared in Tyrol in 1600. They were bred in Nuremberg and later spread throughout Germany, where the Harz Canary originated. This fine songster is kept for its voice, regardless of its colour. In later breeds, aviculturists concentrated on shape, size and coloration.

The staple food consists of four parts sweet rape seed, one part hulled oats and one part canary seed. Occasional supplements are poppyseed, flax and lettuce seed or niger seed. Canaires are also fed apples, figs and other fruit, lettuce, spinach, radishes, unripe plantain spikes and chickweed, and carrots are appreciated. Moulting birds must be given egg mixture, which is also served to females every other day starting in January.

Canaries begin to nest in March. Pairs are kept in a cage which should be at least 50 by 40 by 40 centimetres large. The platform for the nest is either situated inside the cage or suspended on the outside. Canaries are provided with their traditional building materials, such as threads pulled out of pieces of cloth and pieces of stuffing. The female begins sitting as soon as the first egg is laid, and the eggs should be replaced by artificial ones and returned after the fourth egg is laid. This ensures that all the young hatch at the same time, after 13 days. They are fledged after 18 to 20 days.

The yellow-green wild ancestor of the Canary breeds now available inhabits forests, vineyards and road alleys in the Canary Islands, except the island of Fuertaventura. The first yellow singing Canaries (1) were obtained by crossbreeding wild Canaries with Serins (*Serinus serinus*). The first variant, having an erect stance and tall legs (the so-called stance Canary), was probably the Belgian 'Malinois'. The other stance Canaries were bred in Holland and France. Most crossbreeding experiments were undertaken by the English, who developed some well-known breeds of Canaries based on stance: Yorkshire (2), Border Fancy (3), Frill (4), Norwich (5) and Humpback (6). In the twenties, a red-coloured Canary (7) was obtained by crossbreeding with the finch *Spinus cucullatus* from Venezuela and Trinidad.

Red-crested Finch

Fringillidae

Coryphospingus cristatus

The Red-crested Finch is one of the most ornamental birds in the family Fringillidae. Several species of the genus are imported, but their behaviour and treatment in captivity are almost the same.

The diet is millet, canary seed and hulled oats, with a little poppy-seed and rape seed, and an abundance of green food. They are occasionally given egg mixture and ant cocoons. Hemp seed and meal-worm larvae are served sparsely, because they make the birds over-fat.

Finches confined to small cages, where they lack exercise, suffer spasmodic fits. It is therefore advisable to keep them in an indoor or outdoor aviary. The outdoor aviary should be planted with shrubs in which the birds can build their nest. Sometimes they will use a Canary-type cage or a small nestbox with an uncovered top. This species has an interesting courting ritual: the male hops around the female, erects his crest, hangs down his wings and raises his tail feathers vertically, all to the accompaniment of a loud, rather unappealing warbling call. The female lays four to six grey-brown-spotted eggs and incubates them for 11 to 12 days. When the young are hatched, the diet should be enriched by egg mixture and insects. The young are fed by both parents and leave the nest after 12 days. They are independent within a month. In the nesting period, Red-crested Finches behave aggressively towards other residents in the aviary.

3 ♂

The Red-crested Finch reaches a length of 13.5 centimetres, of which about 5.7 centimetres is the tail. The dark red male (1) differs conspicuously from the almost brown female (2). When irritated, the male erects his crest (3), which is bright red in the middle. When the crest is folded, only a narrow black stripe can be seen. The crest is absent in the female.

The Red-crested Finch is distributed in South America from Guyana in the north and Peru in the west across Brazil to northern Argentina in the south. It dwells in thickets, where it builds its nest and feeds on thistle seeds. It avoids human settlements.

Orange Weaver

Euplectes franciscana

Ploceidae

The family Ploceidae includes very exotic birds, particularly the males which in their nuptial plumage display a spectacular range of colours. These birds are undemanding and hardy in captivity, and so are suitable for beginners. Their diet is various sorts of millet and green food. In the breeding season this should be supplemented with germinating seeds and insects.

The Orange Weaver can be kept in a cage or aviary. It is gregarious and several pairs can be housed together. The aviculturist must provide enough thick branches or shrubs, in which the males weave their pouch-shaped nests. Long coconut fibres, stalks of grass and bast serve as building materials. The nest is made by the male. If the female approaches an unfinished nest, he hangs himself by his feet at the bottom of the nest, ruffles his feathers, presses his head against his breast and makes strange creaking and hissing sounds. When the female is about to enter the nest for the first time, the male dances around the construction, ruffles his feathers, bends forward and makes tapping sounds by rapidly flapping his wings. After mating, the female arranges the inside of the nest, while the male stays on guard and chases away intruders. The female sits on the eggs very steadily. The newly hatched weavers are naked except for some down on the head. They open their eyes after 6 days and leave the nest after 13 days. They can fend for themselves by the age of 4 weeks, when they resemble the female.

This species is 11 to 12 centimetres long. The male in his nuptial dress (1) strikingly differs from the predominantly brown female (2).

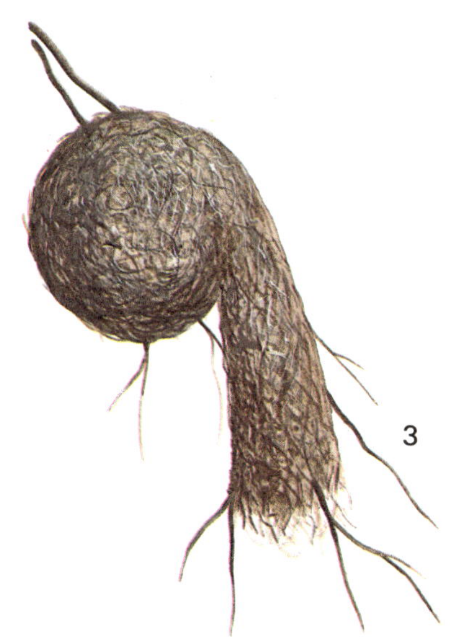

Orange Weavers occur in two subspecies in Africa, from the southern Sahara to northern Cameroon, Central African Republic, the Sudan, northern Uganda, Ethiopia and Somalia. They live in large flocks and following overpopulation, they sometimes raid the millet fields of local inhabitants. They spend the night in reed beds in extensive swamps. At the onset of the breeding season, the males assume their nuptial coloration. The nesting takes place after the rainy season, when the flocks break up into smaller groups and the males build nests (3) in small colonies.

1 ♂

Red-billed Weaver
Quelea quelea

Ploceidae

The Red-billed Weaver is the most frequently imported species of weaver, appearing in abundance in European shops and markets. It is very undemanding, hardy and easy to feed, being content with millet, chickweed, lettuce leaves and other green food. It can be kept in a cage or aviary, both indoors and outdoors. After acclimatization, it will tolerate temperatures down to 10 degrees Centigrade in winter.

Red-billed Weavers may be kept one pair to a cage, although a group in a roomy aviary produces a better visual effect. The males in a flock quarrel constantly but never hurt one another. Small species of songbirds should not be placed in the same aviary. In captivity, especially if confined to a cage, all weavers grow claws very rapidly and need regular trimming. They require fresh water at all times. The aviary must be provided with bast, hay, coconut and sisal fibres, as the males are enthusiastic nest-builders, even constructing nests in the netting. However, breeding in captivity has been rare so far. The male undertakes the same nuptial dances as other species of weaver, and the number of eggs, length of incubation and fledging are roughly the same as in the Orange Weaver. When the adult birds are feeding their offspring, they should be served germinating seeds and insects.

Adult birds attain a length of 11 to 12 centimetres. The male in his nuptial plumage (1) has a red head mask in contrast to the grey-brown female (2). Outside the breeding season, he is coloured like the female but has a red beak. In her winter plumage, the female has a black beak.

The Red-billed Weaver's area of distribution is very extensive. Four geographic forms live in Africa, ranging from Senegal across northern Cameroon, the Sudan and Ethiopia to Somalia. They also occur in Uganda, eastern Africa to Mozambique and Transvaal, Botswana, Damaraland and Angola. The birds are colonial nesters settling in trees, bushes and reeds. The nests are pouch-shaped (3). Weavers cause considerable damage to fields and plantations. Local ecological research has discovered so far unexplained migrations of large flocks of weavers through the countryside.

Paradise Whydah
Steganura paradisea

African whydahs of the genus *Steganura* are noted for the beauty of the male's nuptial plumage and their interesting breeding biology. Whydahs have long tail feathers and require large cages, indoor glass vitrines or outdoor aviaries. In winter, they are kept at about 10 degrees Centigrade; well-acclimatized birds are able to withstand lower temperatures.

The diet is similar to that of weavers: various sorts of millet, a little canary seed, green food, and occasional ant cocoons, mealworm larvae and other insects. Whydahs are brood parasites. Each male has several females, which deposit their eggs in the nests of other birds. The young do not throw out the other nestlings. The foster parents feed both their own offspring and the young whydahs. Each species of whydah probably seeks a host having the same colour of eggs, throat pattern and arrangement of reflexive papillae in the beak of the young.

Males in breeding plumage should not be placed in the company of other small exotic birds. The smaller birds will be frightened by the whydahs' long swaying tail feathers and sometimes even attacked by the males which, however, become very peaceable as soon as they grow their ordinary plumage. Breeding is difficult because of the Paradise Whydah's brood parasitism, but some successful instances have been reported. The eggs can be given to Bengalese Finches to incubate, and the birds are fed the Nightingale mixture and various insects during the breeding period.

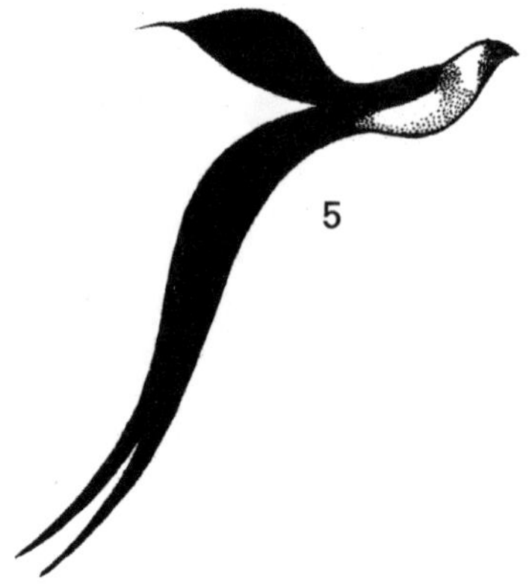

In breeding plumage, the male (1) is very striking, while the female (2) is dull throughout the year. The size is 14 to 15 centimetres excluding the elongated tail feathers, which measure 22 to 26 centimetres. The young have highly developed reflexive papillae in the beak (3). A 16-day-old chick is almost fully feathered (4).

The Paradise Whydah is distributed in six subspecies around the Gulf of Guinea and in central and eastern Africa. The subspecies differ in shape, coloration and length of the male's tail feathers. Paradise Whydahs inhabit open country and hillsides. They live in flocks, often with birds of the family Estrildidae. The females group together, while the males flutter above them (5).

Combassou Ploceidae
Hypochera chalybeata

The Combassou is characterized by distinct dimorphism and interesting brood parasitism. It is an excellent exotic bird for beginners, since it acclimatizes well and is undemanding and easy to feed.

The diet is various sorts of millet (including Senegal millet ears), canary seed, chickweed, lettuce and other green food, and a small quantity of insects. Fresh water for drinking and bathing must be supplied daily. In winter, Combassous are kept at a temperature of about 10 degrees Centigrade.

They do better in indoor or outdoor aviaries than in cages. A male should have three to four females. For breeding purposes, Combassous need the company of Common Fire-finches (*Lagonosticta senegala*), which rear their young. When the finches begin to nest, the Combassou female lays an egg in their nest in the presence of the other female. Common Fire-finches nurse the young Combassous together with their offspring.

Combassous can be housed with various species of waxbills, but the birds have to be watched in the breeding season, when the Combassou becomes aggressive.

The male (1) in breeding plumage is black with a metallic sheen. The female (2) is grey-brown with whitish underparts and resembles the male outside the nesting season. Juvenile birds are greyish brown. The Combassou reaches a length of 10 to 11 centimetres, the wing is 6 centimetres long and the tail measures up to 4 centimetres. The beak of a 12-day-old nestling (3) shows reflexive papillae, and a 16-day-old bird is almost fully feathered (4).

1 ♂

The species occurs in the wild in four subspecies ranging from Senegal across Chad and the Sudan to Ethiopia. The subspecies *H. c. codringtoni* lives in isolation near Lake Malawi. The Combassou's habitat is hillsides and plains, where it forages on the ground. It can be seen in open country, city gardens and streets, village yards, on roofs, and so on.

Orange-cheeked Waxbill
Estrilda melpoda

Estrildidae

This species is imported to Europe in great quantities. It is very active in captivity, always neat and tolerant of other birds. It is an ornamental cage bird, but for breeding it requires ample space in an outdoor or indoor aviary planted with bushes and grass to provide shelter.

Waxbills build a spherical nest with a side entrance and situate it either in thick vegetation on the ground or low down in a bush. A roof should be fitted above the nest so that it is not destroyed by rain. The female lays three to seven eggs and incubates them for 11 to 12 days. When the young are hatched, the parents need to feed them a lot of insects. Insects are easy to find in a densely overgrown outdoor aviary, but the natural diet should be supplemented with fresh ant cocoons, small mealworm larvae, insects gathered by sweeping in the grass, and so on. The birds are also fed various sorts of millet, particularly Senegal millet ears, setaria, canary seed, grass seed, egg mixture and green food. Successful rearing of the young depends on a sufficient supply of animal food. Young waxbills leave the nest after 22 days, and the parent birds feed them for another 14 days. Juvenile birds moult within 6 weeks. Some aviculturists open the aviary in the breeding season, and the birds seek their own food in the surrounding countryside. Waxbills should spend the winter at a temperature of 10 degrees Centigrade.

The male's coloration (1) is the same as the female's. The young (2) are more subdued in colour, the head and underparts are brownish, and the beak is black. The Orange-cheeked Waxbill attains a length of 9 to 10 centimetres.

This species is distributed in three subspecies in western and central Africa, from Senegal and Gambia to Congo. It is a denizen of savannahs, where it settles mainly in the vicinity of rivers and swamps, and on the margins of gallery forests. It is a fast flier, displaying its bright red rump (3) in flight. Waxbills form pairs in the breeding season and afterwards gather in large flocks.

A courting male sings with a stalk in the beak. Waxbills often build a second, unfinished nest above the first one, probably to divert the attention of predators. They behave very cautiously around the real nest and when flushed, they withdraw from it inconspicuously.

1 ♂

Red-eared Waxbill
Estrilda troglodytes

This is probably the most commonly imported species of the family Estrildidae. It was first brought to Europe in the middle of the eighteenth century. Newly imported birds have to undergo gradual acclimatization, but they are basically undemanding, very agile and tolerant of other species.

The Red-eared Waxbill's basic diet is composed of setaria, millet, Senegal millet ears and a little canary seed. The seeds are served both dry and germinating, with a supplement of grasses, plantain, and so on.

They do not usually breed in a cage, preferring an outdoor aviary for nesting. The aviary has to be overgrown with thick bushes and tall grass. The courting male struts before the female with stalk in his beak. The nest is built by both partners low down in a bush or in thick grass. Mating takes place in the nest. The female lays three to eight eggs which are incubated by both partners during the day, and by the female alone at night. The young hatch within 11 to 12 days. They have yellow skin covered by fine bluish down, and distinct blue papillae in the gape. Successful rearing of the brood depends on a nourishing diet. In addition to their basic food, the adult birds must be given fresh ant cocoons, mealworm larvae and a variety of small insects collected by sweeping in a meadow which has not been sprayed by chemicals. Young waxbills leave the nest after 17 to 18 days, and within 14 days males can be distinguished by their twittering. The young moult at the age of 6 weeks.

2 ♀

The beak in the female (2) has a less intense red colour and the red stripe over the eye is slightly narrower and shorter than in the male. The song is a series of notes resembling 'pityui . . . pityui' or 'tyee . . . tyee'; the plain call sounds like 'tee . . . zee'. The nest (3) is spherical, with a covered top and side entrance. The birds sometimes decorate the roof of the nest with conspicuous light-coloured objects such as strips of paper.

The Red-eared Waxbill (1), which reaches a length of 9 to 10 centimetres, lives in the dry steppes of western and eastern Africa, stretching from Senegal and Gambia across the margins of the Sahara to northern Ethiopia. Its occurrence ranges from abundant to sporadic. Waxbills favour low thick bushes on the banks of streams and in marshland.

Common Fire-finch Estrildidae
Lagonosticta senegala

The Common Fire-finch is one of the most readily available species of the family Estrildidae, and it is very popular with aviculturists. Newly imported birds have to be acclimatized with care, particularly the females which are delicate and occur in smaller numbers than the males. The initial temperature of 25 degrees Centigrade is gradually lowered, and after several months the birds will tolerate briefly temperatures around zero, although usually the temperature should not fall below 10 degrees Centigrade.

Common Fire-finches should be situated in a spacious cage or aviary. The aviary should be planted with shrubs on the periphery with the centre left free, because the birds like to move about on the ground. One pair of this species to an aviary is recommended, but other species can be present. The male's call is a whistling note and, when alarmed, a warning 'tsek... tsek'. The courting male hops around the female with a stalk in the beak. The nest is built either in a nestbox or a bush. The clutch numbers four to five white eggs, which are incubated for 11 days. The parents take turns incubating during the day, and the female sits on the clutch at night. Although the adult birds feed their young assiduously, they sometimes throw them out of the nest, which is probably caused by a shortage of animal food. The composition of food has to be checked during the breeding period, as well as the overall activity in the aviary. Juvenile birds are fledged after 17 to 21 days, and their parents feed them for another 14 days, while the young also seek their own food. The basic diet is the same as in the other Estrildidae.

Sexual dimorphism is marked in the Common Fire-finch. The male (1) is predominantly russet-coloured, while the female (2) is pale or dark olive-brown, depending on the subspecies. The length averages 10 centimetres. The juveniles (3) are grey-brown, with a red rump and upper tail coverts, and a grey beak. The gape of a 12-day-old bird shows white reflexive papillae (4). At 16 days, the young are almost fully feathered (5).

The Common Fire-finch is found in some nine geographic forms in most of tropical Africa, from the Sahara and the Nubian Desert to Ethiopia and Somalia, and in eastern Africa as far south as Natal and Transvaal. It is a denizen of dry steppes and savannahs covered with sparse scrub, sometimes reaching the margins of deserts. It prefers living in the vicinity of man (a synanthrophic species).

Cordon Bleu

Uraeginthus bengalus

Estrildidae

This is one of the most popular songbirds of its family owing to its beautiful coloration, liveliness, undemanding way of life and relatively easy breeding. Newly imported birds are delicate and require a warm environment and careful treatment. The males are probably more susceptible to disease than the females, which is unusual in this family of birds. They become hardy after acclimatization and withstand winter temperatures around 0 degrees Centigrade. Their life expectancy in captivity is 12 to 14 years.

The basic diet is various sorts of millet, mainly setaria, Senegal millet ears, a little canary seed and various germinating seeds. Egg mixture is served every other day, together with animal food and chickweed. Since Cordon Bleus tolerate other birds, they can be kept in a large outdoor or indoor aviary. If it is planted with shrubs, the birds build a spherical nest among the branches, mainly on the edges. They will also nest in a box measuring 12 by 12 by 15 centimetres; one third of the box should be open. The clutch is composed of three to seven eggs which both parents take turns incubating for 11 days. The young bird's gape shows azure-blue papillae. In the breeding period, the adult birds need animal food for their offspring, especially ant cocoons, mealworm larvae, *Drosophila* and tiny spiders. The young leave the nest after 20 to 21 days, when they fly with difficulty and move predominantly on the ground.

The male (1) differs from the female (2) in the bold russet spot on the side of his head. The young resemble the female in appearance, but the blue plumage in juvenile males is more intense in colour.

The related species *U. angolensis* (3) is almost identically coloured, except for the half-moon patch on the head of the male. The species *U. cyanocephalus* (4) has an entirely blue head.

The Cordon Bleu is distributed in eight geographic forms in the tropical regions of northern Africa, from Senegal across Cameroon and the Sudan to Ethiopia, Uganda, the highland plateau of Kenya, Tanzania, northern Zimbabwe and Angola. The birds inhabit thorny thickets in the bush and dry steppe areas. They visit ruderal grounds to pick weeds, and in the Ethiopian mountains ascend to a height of 2,400 metres. They live in pairs or small groups, rarely in flocks.

Violet-eared Waxbill
Uraeginthus granatinus

Estrildidae

This beautiful bird is imported to Europe less frequently than the Cordon Bleu. Newly imported birds are highly sensitive to temperature and humidity, and must be kept in a warm and sunny room at a temperature of 20 to 26 degrees Centigrade. Only after several months of acclimatization can the birds withstand sudden changes in temperature.

Experts differ in their opinions regarding breeding in an outdoor aviary. Some rule it out, while others regard it as the only possible way, provided the aviary is sheltered from wind and rain and lets in sunshine. In an overgrown aviary, Violet-eared Waxbills build their nest in a bush or nestbox. The clutch numbers four to six eggs, which are incubated for 14 days. If the pair will not sit steadily, the eggs must be given to Cordon Bleus for incubation and subsequent rearing of the young waxbills. The newly hatched young are buff all over except for the blue rump. After 25 days they begin to assume their adult coloration starting from the head, and the sexes can then be easily distinguished.

Violet-eared Waxbills are fed various sorts of millet, canary seed, a little poppyseed, grass seed and egg mixture. A variety of insects should be served in the breeding period.

The male (1) has black moustaches, chin and throat, and his overall coloration is darker then that of the female (2). The length is 13 to 16 centimetres. It resembles the species *U. ianthinogaster* (3), in which the female (4) has a paler russet head and neck, with a reddish-yellow throat. The coloration of the two sexes, however, is fairly variable.

The Violet-eared Waxbill is native to southern African steppes reaching in the north to the Zambezi River, Botswana, Transvaal and Natal. It frequents scrubland and thin woods, living in pairs or small flocks. Nesting takes place at the end of the rainy season, when food is abundant. The nest is of grass, lined with feathers, and 0.5 to 2.5 metres above ground.

Red-headed Finch (Paradise Sparrow) Estrildidae
Amadina erythrocephala

Imported birds soon acclimatize and become hardy and undemanding but must be protected from freezing temperatures in winter. Some individuals never disturb the other aviary residents, while others harrass them in their nests, often making the birds leave their clutches or broods. Their basic diet is canary seed, dry and germinating millet, occasionally Senegal millet ears, a little poppyseed and egg mixture.

Red-headed Finches can be kept in a roomy cage or aviary. They nest in a nestbox or, exceptionally, build their own nest in a bush. The clutch comprises four to six eggs incubated by both parents. The nesting birds should not be inspected because this might make them leave the clutch. When a sitting female is incidentally disturbed, she ruffles her feathers, stands up and turns her head around. Some pairs are bad sitters and in these cases a maximum of four eggs are given to Bengalese Finches to incubate. The young are hatched after 2 weeks. While they are fed by their parents, small rations of soft and animal food must be served. If the birds are given more than they can consume, they throw the 8- to 10-day-old nestlings out. This behaviour is related to overexcitement of their sexual instinct. Some aviculturists feed the breeding birds only on dry and germinating grain. If the breeding takes a successful course, the young leave the nest after 22 to 24 days, and continue to be fed by their parents for some time.

The male (1) has a brick-red head and throat, while the female's (2) head is greyish brown. A juvenile bird (3) resembles the female but has a black beak. The adult is 13 to 14 centimetres long.

This species is native to southern Africa, where it is distributed from the northern Cape Province across Namibia to southern Angola, Botswana and western Zimbabwe. It inhabits open

country, dry steppes and bushland covered with thorny scrub. The birds often visit human settlements, but they are rather shy. They prefer not to build their own nests, settling instead in the nests vacated by other birds such as weavers and sparrows. Females often lay eggs in nests occupied by a female of the same species, and the clutches are mixed, incubated as a rule by the female who first settled in the nest.

Cut-throat Finch (Ribbon Finch) Estrildidae
Amadina fasciata

This is thought to be the first species of exotic songbirds to be imported to Europe, probably as early as in the seventeenth century. Since then it has been imported in large numbers and is popular for its hardiness and undemanding way of life.

It is fed a mixture of various sorts of millet, setaria, Senegal millet ears, all dry, soaked or germinating. Abundant supplements of green food, egg mixture, calcium and vitamins must be given. Some experts do not advise adding animal food even in the rearing period, while others regard it as essential, especially ant cocoons and mealworm larvae. If used, this food has to be served carefully when the young are fed. If Cut-throat Finches are given food too rich in protein, their sexual instinct becomes overexcited, which makes them throw their young out of the nest and start a new clutch. They sometimes become aggressive and, when they are not nesting, they tend to disturb other birds in their nests. Since pairs differ in behaviour, they should be housed separately in a large cage or aviary. Cut-throat Finches usually breed in a nestbox, but will build a nest in a bush if they are put into an aviary. The female lays four to eight eggs and both parents share incubation for 12 to 14 days. When receiving the right food, the young leave the nest after 21 days, and continue to get additional food from their parents for a long time. As soon as they become entirely independent, they have to be transferred to another aviary, because the parents pursue them.

The length of this species is 12 to 13 centimetres. The male (1) has a carmine-red stripe below the throat and a chestnut-brown spot on the abdomen. The female (2) lacks these features. Juvenile birds resemble their parents, but their colours are more subdued.

The Cut-throat Finch occurs in three subspecies in Africa, ranging from Senegal across the southern Sudan to northern and north-eastern Ethiopia, and down eastern Africa to Transvaal in the south. It frequents dry steppes and semideserts covered by acacias. It is also found in the vicinity of native villages and on the margins of fields. The nests are built in low bushes, trees, on roofs and in tree hollows. Abandoned weavers' nests are sometimes used; they reduce the entry hole and line the nesting chamber.

Golden-breasted Waxbill

Estrildidae

Amandava subflava

This is one of the smallest members of the family Estrildidae. It is very popular with aviculturists because of its undemanding habits, beautiful colours and tolerance of other species of birds. With good treatment, its life expectancy in captivity is up to 10 years. Golden-breasted Waxbills are very fond of bathing and basking in the sun. They are fed small-grained varieties of millet, sĕtaria and Senegal millet ears. They require daily rations of ant cocoons, mealworm larvae or other insects, and egg mixture.

This species thrives best in an outdoor or indoor aviary planted with greenery, mainly bushes. The birds are undemanding in their choice of nest, sometimes building their own nest in a bush. A nestbox measuring 12 by 12 by 12 centimetres is recommended, with half of the front wall open. Vacated nests of other birds are also used. Waxbills need building materials for the nest, such as long stalks of grass and coconut fibres, and feathers for lining the nesting cup. The courting male does not hold a stalk in his beak like other birds of this family; he bends forward before the female, with his tail spread and ruffled. The female lays three to six, exceptionally nine, eggs, which are incubated by both partners for 11 to 12 days. The young stay in the nest for 21 days, and when they leave it, they are sensitive to drops in temperature. In coloration, they resemble young Amaduvade Finches. A variety of insects must be supplied while the young are reared.

The Golden-breasted Waxbill attains a length of 9 centimetres. In the form *A. s. subflava,* the male (3) has an orange-coloured breast and abdomen, and a red stripe above the eye. The female (4) lacks this stripe and her underparts are pale yellow in the middle. The male of *A. s. clarkei* (1) is pale yellow from the beak to the lower tail coverts, and the female (2) resembles the hen in the nominate form, but her abdomen is yellower.

It occurs in two subspecies distributed in Africa from Senegal to Ethiopia, ranging south to Transvaal, Natal and the northern Cape Province. In the wild, this species inhabits steppes, coastal regions and marshland. In Ethiopia, it ascends to a height of 2,500 metres. It often nests in colonies, sometimes using nests abandoned by weavers. Outside the breeding season, populations of Golden-breasted Waxbills form large flocks.

Amaduvade Finch
Amandava amandava

Estrildidae

The Amaduvade Finch is the only species of its family to have special nuptial plumage during the breeding season. It is very hardy and undemanding and, when treated well, it can live up to 10 years. Acclimatization of imported birds is not difficult and after it the finches can withstand mild freezing weather, although it is inadvisable to expose them to frost. They need ample sunshine and like to bask in the Sun's rays. If kept in a dark and moist place, their colours become dark. Their diet is millet, setaria, Senegal millet ears, and chickweed.

This species can breed even in a cage, but an outdoor or indoor aviary planted with bushes and grass or reeds and rushes is preferable; the birds climb the plants and so trim their claws in a natural way. The nest is built in grass underneath a thick bush, in a nestbox or a Canary-type cage. The clutch numbers four to six, sometimes nine eggs. Incubation is shared by both parents. The young hatch after 12 to 14 days and insects are a vital component of their diet. Insects are collected by sweeping in a meadow where chemical sprays are not used. The basic animal food for the young consists of mealworm larvae and ant cocoons. Egg mixture is a good supplement. The young leave the nest after 3 weeks and begin to moult after another 3 weeks, the change of plumage taking 3 months.

3

The male in his nuptial plumage (1) is predominantly purple-red with white spots. The female (2) is brownish above and ochre-yellow below. The young are like the female in appearance but have a black beak (3). The length is 9 to 10 centimetres.

Three subspecies of the Amaduvade Finch are found in the wild. The nominative subspecies *A. a. amandava* lives in central, western and southern India, eastern Pakistan and eastern Assam. The subspecies *A. a. punicea* is native to Indochina, Java, Bali, inland Thailand, Cambodia and Hainan. *A. a. flavidiventris* is resident in the islands of Lombok, Sumba, Flores and Timor, and in Burma. In the nesting season, Amaduvade Finches live in pairs and sometimes in colonies. After the fledging of the young they gather in large flocks.

2 ♀
1 ♂

Blue-faced Finch
Erythrura trichroa

Estrildidae

The Blue-faced Finch was first brought to Europe in 1886 and bred successfully in 1887. It is a highly mobile and lively bird, which should be kept in an aviary planted with greenery rather than in a cage.

It is fed millet, canary seed and oats, both dry and germinating. This diet is supplemented with egg mixture, animal food, fruit and green food.

Pairs thrive in an aviary and nest and breed readily. The courting ritual is very animated: the male pursues the female in fast flight, pinches her nape with his beak, and then mating takes place. The nest is usually built in a half-open nestbox measuring 12 by 12 by 15 centimetres. In an overgrown aviary, the birds build the nest in a bush. The clutch comprises four to five eggs measuring 15 by 10 millimetres. Incubation is carried out by the female during the day and by both partners at night. In the daytime, the male guards the nest from unwelcome visitors. The young hatch within 12 to 14 days and leave the nest after 22 to 24 days. The parents bring them additional food for another 2 weeks. Adult coloration is assumed after 3 months.

The song is a series of sharp, trilling notes sounding like 'tsit-tsit-tsit'. After good acclimatization (particularly in birds kept for generations in European conditions), Blue-faced Finches can withstand a temperature of 0 degrees Centigrade, for short periods of time. Since this species breeds readily, it is used by aviculturists to rear the rarer species of finches of the genus *Erythrura.*

Trichroa, or 'tricoloured', is descriptive of the colour combination of the Blue-faced Finch's plumage. The male's feathers (1) are bright green, blue and red. In the female (2), these colours are duller, especially on the head. Juvenile birds (3) are olive-green below, the blue colour on the head is absent or very subdued, and the beak is paler.

The Blue-faced Finch's area of distribution covers an extensive territory, within which several geographic forms are distinguished. They live in the Moluccas, New Guinea, Solomon Islands, New Hebrides, Caroline Islands, Bismarck Archipelago, and on the eastern coast of the Australian York Peninsula. They frequent locations near water, both in lowlands and mountains, and tend to become synanthropic, i.e. prefer living in the vicinity of man.

2 ♀

1 ♂

Parrot Finch
Erythrura psittacea

Estrildidae

For many decades, the Parrot Finch has been one of the most popular species in the family Estrildidae. Careful treatment in a suitable environment results in successful breeding and rearing of the young. Newly imported birds are acclimatized at a minimum temperature of 20 degrees Centigrade. Birds bred in Europe are resistant to cold and changes in weather, and throughout the winter, they are kept at an average temperature of 10 degrees Centigrade.

Since Parrot Finches are very animated, it is advisable to place them in an indoor aviary or glass vitrine rather than a cage. They are very fond of bathing. The diet consists of canary seed, mixed sorts of millet, a little niger seed, ant cocoons, quality egg mixture, green food, fruit, calcium, vitamins and trace elements. Germinating seeds must be added throughout the year. Feeding too much oily seeds and meal-worm larvae must be avoided, since it will cause the birds to become fat and suffer liver diseases.

Breeding succeeds best in an aviary planted with bushes and other greenery. Several pairs should be housed together. The male brings the building material in tufts and wisps, which is exceptional among the Estrildidae. The nest is built in a bush or situated in a half-open nestbox, and lined with feathers or fine grass. The female lays four to five eggs, which are incubated by both parents for 13 to 14 days. The young leave the nest after 20 to 21 days and assume their adult coloration within 4 months. The male's song sounds like 'tri-tri-tri-tri-ri-ri-ri-i-i-i'.

3

1 ♂

This species attains a length of 12 to 13 centimetres. The male (1) has a strikingly red head. The female (2) has a slightly longer beak and the red colour on the head is not as extensive. Juvenile birds (3) resemble the female but lack the glossy sheen. Young males usually have a redder head than females.

The Parrot Finch is restricted in the wild to the islands of New Caledonia. It seeks bush-covered grassland. The spherical nest is usually built in trees, sometimes in rocks and buildings. Pairs are formed in the nesting season, and at other times populations of Parrot Finches merge in flocks. They feed chiefly on grass seeds.

Gouldian Finch

Erythrura gouldiae

This is one of the most beautiful species of bird. It was described in 1844 by the English ornithologist and painter John Gould. The Gouldian Finch is highly sensitive to drops in temperature, and should be kept in a large indoor vitrine or glass cage. In Europe the ideal ambient temperature is 24 degrees Centigrade and above, and the relative humidity should be 65 to 70 per cent. The higher the temperature, the higher the atmospheric humidity can be, and vice versa.

Gouldian Finches are fed a mixture composed of 30 per cent setaria or millet, 30 per cent canary seed, 30 per cent Senegal millet and 10 per cent white millet. Germinating ears of Senegal millet can also be served. Some individuals take a long time to get used to egg mixture and animal food, but they appreciate raw eggs. The diet must be supplemented with minerals, trace elements and vitamins. Some aviculturists recommend a weekly ration of cod-liver oil in winter.

The best size for the nestbox is 15 by 15 by 15 centimetres. A variety of building material should be available, since each pair has their preference. Dog grass (*Agrostis*), for instance, is a suitable material. Some pairs line the nestbox very sparsely, and it has to be adjusted by the keeper. The clutch numbers four to eight eggs measuring 17 by 13 millimetres. Incubation is carried out by both parents for 14 to 16 days. The adult birds feed their young on predigested, regurgitated food from the crop. The young are fledged after 22 to 24 days. If the eggs or nestlings are neglected by their parents they can be given to Bengalese Finches.

This species attains a length of 14 centimetres. The female (2) is coloured like her partner, but her plumage lacks his lustre, and the middle tail feathers are shorter. There are several forms which differ in the colour of the head. Perhaps the most beautiful is the red-headed form (1). There are three times as many black-headed Gouldian Finches (3) in the wild as red-headed ones. Approximately one bird per 5,000 Gouldian Finches is yellow-headed (4). The gape of the young shows a white protuberance and two blue papillae (5) in the corners; their gullet is also interesting (6).

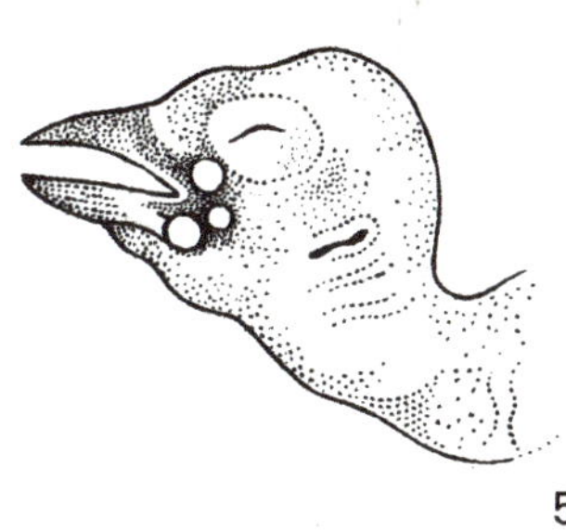

The Gouldian Finch is confined to the northern tropical region of Australia except the eastern part of the York Peninsula. It inhabits hot dry savannahs and it nests in hollow trees, abandoned termite mounds and vacated birds' nests in cavities. Exceptionally, a flimsy nest in the grass or in a bush is constructed.

Diamond Firetail

Estrildidae

Emblema guttata

The Diamond Firetail is elegant in coloration, hardy and undemanding, and will grace any aviculturist's collection. In Europe, this species has been bred since the early nineteenth century.

The diet is millet, setaria, canary seed and a little hemp seed from time to time. The seeds are served both dry and germinating, and the diet is supplemented with green food, such as chickweed and shepherd's purse and egg mixture. Insects caught in an entomological net are served together with mealworm larvae and ant cocoons, particularly during the breeding season. Fresh drinking water must be regularly supplied. Diamond Firetails drink like pigeons, sucking water without lifting their head.

Several pairs can be housed in a large aviary, but in a smaller space the birds disturb one another. Branches of pine, fir and spruce should be affixed at various levels on the walls or in the corners of an outdoor aviary. A large spherical nest is built among the branches from thin birch twigs, grass stalks, straw, sisal fibres, feathers, and so on. A nestbox is used if no suitable place for a nest is found. The courting male holds a grass stalk in the beak, inflates his body, moves his head forward and sideways, rocks up and down and makes a deep, buzzing sound. The female lays four to seven white eggs measuring 18 by 13 millimetres. The young hatch within 14 to 15 days and leave the nest after 22 to 25 days. At 4 to 6 months, juvenile birds begin to grow their adult plumage. Some pairs are unreliable sitters and their clutch is given to Bengalese Finches, which should not, however, rear more than two to three young Diamond Firetails.

2

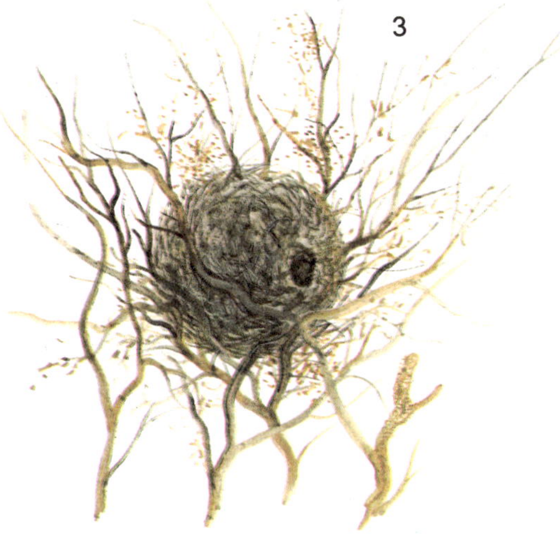

The Diamond Firetail (1) reaches a length of 12 centimetres, but looks bigger and more robust. The male's deep and quiet song is the only way of distinguishing the sexes. The juveniles (2) are grey-brown with an indistinct pattern and black beak.

The home of this species is in south-eastern Australia, in the bush and grassland steppe sparsely covered with trees and bushes. The covered nest is built in tall bushes or trees. It is 24 to 30 centimetres long, 10 to 20 centimetres high and 12 to 17 centimetres wide (3), lined with feathers. There are, as a rule, two broods in the wild.

Crimson Finch
Neochmia phaeton

Estrildidae

The Crimson Finch is a very handsome and elegant songbird, particularly the male with its glossy red plumage. This species is rarely sold, because newly imported individuals are delicate and require warmth and care, although they become hardy after acclimatization. During the summer, Crimson Finches can be kept in a spacious outdoor aviary overgrown with bushes, or in a glasshouse aviary. If they lack space, they tend to quarrel with other species of their family. They are fed millet, setaria, Senegal millet and other grass seeds, which are served dry, sometimes half-ripe. Good supplements are egg mixture, mealworm larvae and ant cocoons. Small insects gathered by sweeping are welcome mainly when the young are reared, although animal food is essential throughout the year. They also need plenty of calcium and vitamins A, D_2, B and C.

The birds breed in an indoor aviary planted with an abundance of evergreen potted shrubs. The nest is built in a bush or in a nestbox measuring 12 by 12 by 15 centimetres. Hay, dry leaves and feathers are needed for the construction. The clutch comprises five to eight white eggs 14 by 12 millimetres large. Incubation is performed by both partners during the day and by the female alone at night. The young hatch after 16 days and leave the nest when they are 21 days old. They are then fed for some time by the male, while the female usually starts a new clutch. Young birds change colour at 6 months of age.

2 ♀

The Crimson Finch occurs in three geographic forms. The nominative subspecies *N. p. phaeton* lives in north-western Australia. The male's (1) dazzling red colour can be seen from afar. The female (2) only has red on the throat and sides of the head. The subspecies *N. p. iredalei* inhabits Queensland in the north-east. *N. p. albiventer* (3) is found in the northernmost part of the York Peninsula and in the south of New Guinea.

These birds live predominantly in small groups. Their ideal haunts are marshlands, but they can be encountered in dry locations as well, often in the margins of sugar-cane plantations. They build a spherical nest with an entrance 13 centimetres long. It is usually situated in *Pandanus* trees or underneath eaves, on telegraph poles and so on.

3 ♂

Star Finch
Bathilda ruficauda

Estrildidae

The Star Finch, attractively coloured, lively and undemanding, has become a great favourite with aviculturists in recent years. It is always tolerant of other birds in the aviary, adapts easily to a new environment, and soon becomes tame. Its call resembles 'slit-slit' and the song is a weak twittering. The basic diet is millet, setaria, canary seed and Senegal millet ears, all served dry and germinating. This is supplemented with egg mixture, green food, ant cocoons, mealworm larvae and other small insects. Sufficient rations of calcium and vitamin D have to be supplied. When Star Finches are rearing their young, the percentage of animal food must be increased.

The Star Finch can be kept in a cage or in an indoor or outdoor aviary. A nestbox inside a cage should measure 12 by 12 by 15 centimetres, with half of the front wall open. In an aviary, the birds build a simple nest in a bush or among reeds, which should be planted there for this purpose. They prefer to use fresh grass as building material because of its strength. The male holds a stalk of grass in his beak while courting the female and performing his ritual nuptial dance. After mating, the female lays three to six eggs measuring 15 by 11 millimetres. The parents take turns incubating them for 12 to 14 days. The young leave the nest after 20 days, but they are not fully independent and have to be fed by the adults for a long time. The nestlings can be reared by Bengalese Finches, but there will be some problems with the feeding of the fledged young.

The maximum length of a Star Finch is 12 centimetres. The male (1) is olive-buff, with a red head mask. The female (2) is almost identically coloured, but the red mask is less extensive and the underparts are paler, with less pronounced white dots. The juvenile bird (3) has a yellow-grey head, yellow-brown eyes and a black beak.

This species inhabits northern and north-western Australia. It lives in scrubland, tall grass and reed beds, where it feeds mainly on grass seed. It moves around in small flocks and forms pairs in the nesting season. The nest is built in grass or bushes, and is spherical or bottle-shaped, with a side entrance.

2 ♀

1 ♂

Black-ringed Finch (Double-barred Finch) Estrildidae
Stizoptera bichenovii

This species was brought to Europe in 1870. It is a lively, tolerant and elegantly coloured bird. With good treatment, these finches breed freely not only in an indoor or outdoor aviary, but also in a large cage. However, they cannot tolerate chilly and humid conditions, which will cause intestinal catarrhs and death. They thrive best in sunny aviaries.

The diet is composed of millet, setaria and Senegal millet ears. The seeds are served both dry and germinating. Egg mixture and green food are added daily, and a few mealworm larvae, ant cocoons and insects obtained by sweeping are occasionally supplied. Animal food is the staple diet of the young. In winter, vitamins are dissolved in drinking water or added to soft food. The birds also need plenty of calcium.

The male's call is a loud and long 'tyaaat-tyaat' and a short, nasal 'tut-tut'. When courting the female, the male runs around his mate in half-circles and sings. Mating takes place on the ground. The nest is built in a bush or in a nestbox 12 by 12 by 15 centimetres. The female lays four to six white eggs measuring 16 by 12 millimetres. The young hatch within 11 days, and leave the nest after 22 to 25 days. They continue to be fed for another 14 days. The parents then begin to pursue them and the young have to be transferred. They assume their adult coloration at 6 to 10 weeks of age.

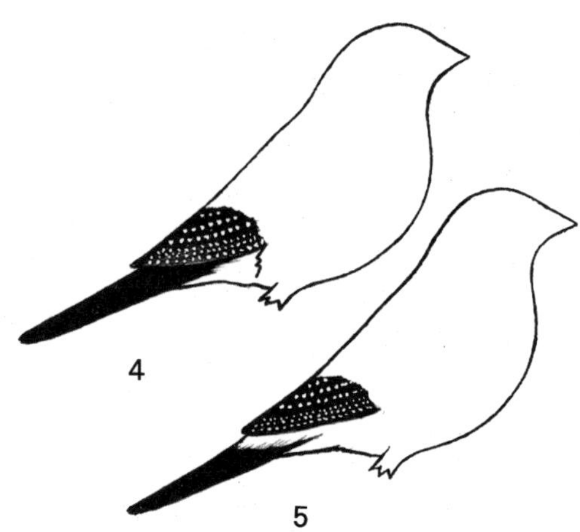

The Black-ringed Finch (1) attains a length of 11 centimetres. It occurs in two subspecies in northern and eastern Australia. The nominative subspecies *S. b. bichenovii* is found in the east. The male (2) differs from the female (3) only slightly. She usually has white underparts with a very narrow band across the breast. The subspecies *S. b. annulosa* lives in the north-west; it has a black rump (4), unlike the nominative form in which the rump is white (5). The birds live in small groups in savannahs covered with thick bushes and scattered trees. They seek the vicinity of water and forage for grass seed on the ground. The spherical nest is built in thick grass or low down in bushes.

Zebra Finch

Estrildidae

Taeniopygia guttata

Among small songbirds, the Zebra Finch is the most frequently kept species, and also the cheapest one. It is hardy and breeds freely, and is, therefore, an ideal cage bird for beginners. It is extremely lively and should be placed in an aviary rather than a cage.

The diet is simple, based on millet, setaria, canary seed and Senegal millet, all served both dry and germinating. Egg mixture, chickweed and green food are added, with occasional ant cocoons, mealworm larvae, sponge and white bread soaked in milk. Vitamins and calcium are important supplements. The birds need plenty of sunshine, and fresh water for drinking and bathing.

In a cage or indoor aviary, Zebra Finches nest readily in virtually any season. They are given nestboxes with a half-open front wall, and building materials. The female lays four to five, sometimes eight, white eggs with a green sheen, measuring 11 by 15 millimetres. The young hatch within 11 days, grow fast and leave the nest in less than 3 weeks. They begin to change colour at the age of 5 to 6 weeks and have adult coloration at 2 months, when the males and females are separated. The young are not allowed to breed until they are 1 year old. Zebra Finches are sometimes used to rear the offspring of some rare birds of the family Estrildidae.

The call resembles sounds made by a children's trumpet and is finished by a short and soft repetitive 'tet'. The song is composed of harsh nasal trills lasting 1 to 2 seconds.

The male (1) differs in colour from the predominantly grey female (2). The young (3) resemble the female, but they are dark brown, with a black beak. It attains a length of 10 centimetres.

A white mutation (4) was bred in 1921 and others followed, for example, silver (5), mottled (6) and black-breasted (7).

There are two subspecies: the nominative form *T. g. guttata* inhabits the Lesser Sunda Islands, such as Flores, Sumba, Timor and some smaller ones. The subspecies *T. g. castanotis* (1, 2) is widespread throughout Australia except the south-western tip, the northernmost Northern Territory, the York Peninsula and the coastal areas of Victoria and New South Wales. In the Australian countryside, the Zebra Finch is a denizen of open dry country covered with scrub and solitary trees. The bottle-shaped nest has an entrance up to 25 centimetres long.

Black-throated Finch Estrildidae
Poephila acuticauda

This bird was discovered and described by the painter John Gould in 1839. At present, Black-throated Finches bred in Europe are regularly marketed. Although they are not very sensitive to cold, they must be installed in heated quarters during the winter months. They get along relatively well with other birds of their family, but in the breeding season they may become agressive and if so, should be transferred. Black-throated Finches do well in a cage or aviary.

They are fed millet, setaria, canary seed and Senegal millet ears. Half-ripe grass seed, chickweed and similar food are served in season. The birds must be given calcium and animal food, especially when rearing their young. The call is a long 'thwirr' and a short 'tet'. The song is a flute-like whistle and a bubbling phrase.

The nest is often built in a nestbox, preferably 12 by 12 by 12 centimetres. Hay, sisal and coconut fibres are supplied as building materials. In an aviary, a covered nest is sometimes built in a bush. It is 20 centimetres long, 13 centimetres high and 11 centimetres wide, with a tunnel-shaped entrance 7.5 centimetres long. Four to six white eggs measuring 16 by 12 millimetres form the usual clutch. Most pairs incubate their eggs steadily in captivity, but they often fail to rear the brood. In such cases, the eggs or nestlings are given to Bengalese Finches. The young leave the nest after 21 days. Until they assume their adult coloration, they are sensitive to change of environment and disturbance.

There are two subspecies. *P. a. hecki* (1), a red-beaked form, inhabits the north-eastern part of the Australian Northern Territory. The yellow-beaked subspecies *P. a. acuticaudata* (2) lives in the western regions of northern Australia. The Black-throated Finch reaches a length of 15 centimetres. The sexes are almost identical in appearance. In 1-year-old specimens, the female's (3) black bib is slightly smaller than that of the male. The gape of young birds shows reflexive papillae (4).

In the wild, the Black-throated Finch frequents savannahs sparsely covered with eucalyptus trees. It builds its nest in their crowns. In places where trees are absent, the birds nest in bushes or grass tufts. The partners are extremely devoted; they always sit close to one another, mutually preen their feathers and move everywhere together.

3 ♀

1 ♂

Java Sparrow (Rice-bird)

Padda oryzivora

Estrildidae

Reports on this popular bird date from 1790. Among the best-suited species for keeping in a cage, it is hardy and undemanding, and breeds readily. Java Sparrows are peaceable birds but should not be housed in the same cage with smaller exotic birds. Newly imported individuals remain shy for a long time. The birds are fond of bathing, and they are always smooth and neat. Throughout winter, they are kept in heated quarters at low temperatures.

The diet is various sorts of millet, canary seed, unhulled oats, and, in season, green ears of wheat. Germinating seeds can be served as well. Green food is supplied daily and egg mixture is given from time to time. When rearing their young, the birds are given more egg mixture, supplemented with fresh ant cocoons and mealworm larvae.

The nest is usually built in a nestbox measuring 15 by 15 by 18 centimetres, with the front wall half open. In an aviary, the pair builds a large, spherical, untidy nest affixed to a wall or among branches. Grass, straw, hay, bast, coconut fibres and so on should be supplied as building materials. Java Sparrows are not very particular and use any material that is available. The female lays four to eight eggs and the young hatch within 13 to 14 days, leave the nest after 4 weeks and continue to receive food from their parents for another 14 days. As soon as they become independent, they have to be separated from the adults who begin to pursue them. Under favourable conditions, juvenile birds assume their adult coloration within 2 to 3 months.

The Java Sparrow is 13.5 centimetres long. The male (1) has the same simple but elegant appearance as the female, although she has a more slender head and paler beak (2). The juvenile bird (3) is dark grey above and pale yellow-grey below, with a black beak. A white form with black eyes (4), which was bred several centuries ago in China and Japan, still exists.

This species is native to Indonesia, where it is distributed from Sumatra across Java to the Moluccas. It was introduced by humans to Zanzibar and

the Island of St Helen. Captive birds which escaped started new populations in eastern Africa, south-eastern Asia, Japan and Hawaii. In their homeland, Java Sparrows live in steppes and agricultural regions, where they cause heavy damage in rice paddies outside the breeding season.

1 ♂

Three-coloured Mannikin Estrildidae
Lonchura malacca

A regularly imported bird, it becomes hardy after acclimatization and tolerates the company of other birds. It can be kept in a cage or aviary, both indoors and outdoors. The song is mediocre and very quiet.

The diet is simple, consisting mainly of millet, setaria and egg mixture, although some birds do not take egg food. They like unripe or germinating seeds, chickweed and green food.

Some pairs fail to breed in captivity. For breeding purposes, it is advisable to place the birds in an aviary and plant it with shrubs, reeds, rushes or other tall grasses. Both partners take part in building the spherical nest of couch-grass, bast, roots, dry grass, straw and pine needles, which should be supplied. Sometimes they settle in a nestbox measuring 12 by 12 by 15 centimetres, with the front wall half open. The courting male chases the female and hops around with his feathers ruffled, bending his head down and singing. The clutch comprises three to six eggs and the young are hatched after 14 days. They grow quickly, particularly if the parents are supplied with a rich variety of food. Most birds do not mind inspection of the nest. Young birds are fledged after 3 weeks and can fend for themselves after another 2 weeks. They assume their adult coloration at the age of 6 months. Crossbreeding has been undertaken with the Bengalese Finch, Zebra Finch and several species of mannikin.

This species reaches a length of 11 to 12 centimetres. The most frequently imported subspecies is *L. m. malacca* (1). The sexes are alike in appearance, and their back (2) is brown.

The Three-coloured Mannikin is distributed in some nine subspecies throughout India and Indochina, southern China, the Sunda Islands, the Philippines

and Indonesia. It lives in reed beds and tall grass. In agricultural regions, the birds concentrate in rice paddies and sugar-cane plantations. The nest (3) is spherical or bottle-shaped, built at various heights in trees and bushes. After fledging, the young stay in flocks with their parents. In some localities, there are large flocks outside the nesting season.

3

Spice Finch (Nutmeg Mannikin) Estrildidae
Lonchura punctulata

This readily available species is quiet, tolerant of other aviary residents, and very hardy after acclimatization. The diet is various sorts of millet, canary seed and setaria; the seeds are served dry or germinating. Egg mixture, green food, ant cocoons and mealworm larvae are supplied every other day. The rations of animal food must be increased in the breeding season.

The Spice Finch can be kept either in a cage or in any type of aviary. Breeding in captivity used to be a rarity but nowadays there is a strong European breeding stock, which multiplies with success. In an aviary overgrown with plants, Spice Finches build a nest in a bush. They will also settle in a nestbox. The female lays four to seven white eggs measuring 17 by 12 millimetres, and both parents take turns incubating them for 13 days. The dark brown young have paler underparts and a horseshoe pattern on the upper palate of the beak. They leave the nest after 3 weeks. The change to adult coloration takes 6 months, and is affected by temperature, light intensity, atmospheric humidity and composition of food. Some bird-keepers use this species to rear some rare species of firetail, even if they have never had a brood before. As a rule, they look after the other young with great care. Spice Finches have been crossbred with several species of Estrildidae and most often with Bengalese Finches.

The Spice Finch (1) is 11 centimetres long. The males and females are identical. Dark brown rings can be seen on their underparts in flight (2).

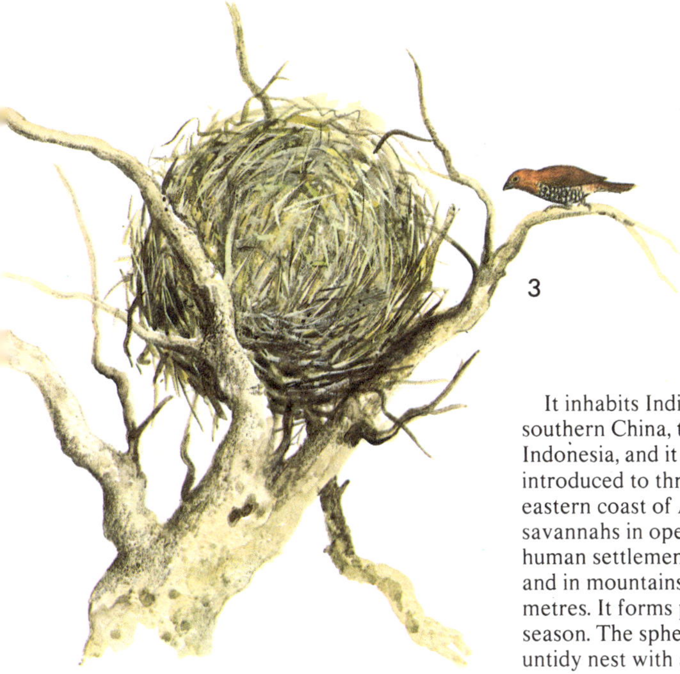

It inhabits India and Indochina, southern China, the Malay Peninsula, Indonesia, and it was successfully introduced to three localities on the eastern coast of Australia. Its habitat is savannahs in open country, or areas near human settlements. It occurs in lowlands and in mountains up to a height of 2,000 metres. It forms pairs in the breeding season. The spherical, relatively large, untidy nest with a side entrance (3) is built 1.5 to 12 metres above the ground, usually in thorny bushes. The call sounds like 'kit-leh', and the alarm call is 'kchep'.

Bengalese Finch
Estrildidae

Lonchura domestica

The Bengalese Finch is an invaluable aid to an aviculturist since it willingly tends the eggs or broods of some rare songbirds of the family Estrildidae, which refuse to incubate their clutches in captivity. It is very undemanding, and is, therefore, a suitable bird for laymen and beginners. It tolerates all small birds, but it can be harassed by a very small attacker, and it is advisable to keep a pair separately. A cage is preferable to an aviary. In winter, Bengalese Finches must have a frost-free environment. They are very fond of bathing. The diet is a mixture of various sorts of millet, a little canary seed, occasional egg mixture, sponge, green food and fruit.

Bengalese Finches prefer to nest in a box, with the half of the front wall open, measuring roughly 12 by 12 by 12 centimetres. They line the nest with hay and similar material. The female lays three to eight eggs which both parents take turns incubating during the day, while at night they sit on them together. The young hatch after 12 days and leave the nestbox after a further 21 days. The parents feed them for another 8 to 12 days. Once they become independent, the young have to be put in another cage, because otherwise they sleep in the nestbox and disturb the adults sitting on a second clutch. Bengalese Finches should be kept one pair to a cage because the gregarious birds would all tend to sleep in the same nestbox. Although the juveniles become sexually mature early, they should not be used for breeding purposes until they are over 8 months old. A pair should not be allowed to have more than three broods a year.

2

The Bengalese Finch, measuring some 13 centimetres when adult, was created many centuries ago in Japan by the crossbreeding of several related species of mannikin. The basic species used for breeding were probably the Striated Finch (*Lonchura striata*), Sharp-tailed Munia (*Lonchura acuticaudata*), and the Indian Silverbill (*Euodice malabarica*).

1

The male Bengalese Finch can be recognized by his monotonous song. When singing, he raises the head and stretches the neck. Coloration is highly variable. The original Bengalese Finches were mottled dark brown (1) or pale brown. Many varieties have been bred, for example, dark brown with white underparts (2), yellow (3), white (4), rusty (5).

African Silverbill
Euodice cantans

Estrildidae

Since 1776, when the African Silverbill was first brought to Europe, it has been sold regularly and in great quantities. It is a very hardy bird, usually tolerant of other species, and therefore suitable for beginners. The male's brief but pleasant song can be heard most of the time. The African Silverbill can be kept in any type of cage or aviary, but an outdoor aviary is best in the summer months. In winter, sufficiently acclimatized birds can be housed in a room with a temperature of 10 degrees Centigrade.

The diet consists of millet, canary seed, chickweed and egg mixture. Breeding takes place in either a nestbox or a basket. The courting male dances with a stalk in the beak. The female lays three to six eggs and incubates them for 11 to 12 days. The newly hatched young are naked, having a greyish violet skin. Animal food must be supplied in the rearing period. The young leave the nest after 3 weeks if they are fed well. They change plumage within 5 to 8 weeks. Young males can be recognized early by their singing attempts.

The African Silverbill nests readily but does not always rear its offspring. This depends on the pair and on the living conditions. A good pair will rear up to twenty-five young in a season. Some pairs do not tolerate inspection of the nest; it frightens them and often causes them to leave the clutch. The African Silverbill can be crossbred easily with some species of finch and firetail and with the Bengalese Finch.

An adult bird is 11 centimetres long. The male (1) is similar to the female, but the base of his beak is wider. The juveniles are dark grey-brown, with paler underparts and a black beak.

The African Silverbill is distributed in northern Africa from Senegal to the Red Sea, and in eastern Africa south to central Tanzania. It also lives in south-western Arabia. In the wild, it always seeks dry localities. It forms pairs in the nesting season and can be found in the vicinity of human settlements. The nest is built in thorny bushes, and in some regions, the Silverbill settles in nests abandoned by weavers. A similar species, the Indian Silverbill (*E. malabarica*) (2), has a white rump and upper tail coverts, and lives in India, south-eastern Iran, Afghanistan, West Pakistan and Bangladesh.

Shama
Copsychus malabaricus

The Shama is one of the few birds kept chiefly for their singing. It is one of the best songsters, having a more varied repertoire than the Nightingale (*Luscinia megarhynchos*). Each individual sings differently and has its own composition. The song is pure and very strong, and some people prefer to listen to it from an adjoining room. Some Shamas, however, turn out to be disappointing songsters. A male has to be situated in a large cage, because its tail feathers are up to 16 centimetres long.

The Shama is fed the Thrush mixture, supplemented with large insects and mealworm larvae. A pair kept in a roomy outdoor or indoor aviary will breed readily. It is not advisable to keep small songbirds of the family Estrildidae in the company of Shamas, because they could easily be killed by them. The pair usually builds their nest in a nestbox measuring 20 by 20 by 15 centimetres, with the front wall half open. The female lays two to six eggs and the young hatch after 13 days. At first they are fed by the female and after 5 days by both parents. The adults consume large quantities of insects during this time. The young leave the nest 14 days after hatching, but the parents partly feed them for another 3 weeks. Young males begin to sing when they are 6 weeks old. A Shama will live for 15 to 20 years if it is treated well.

This species attains a length of 28 centimetres. The male (1) is blackish blue with a metallic sheen above, the underparts are chestnut-brown, and the rump is white. The female (2) is olive-brown above and pale brown below. The syrinx (vocal organ) is highly developed in the male. The cartilaginous structure of the vocal organ (3) has a drum in the upper part and tracheal cartilages in the wide central part. In a cross-section of the syrinx (4), the vocal muscles are shown in a dark colour, the tracheal cartilage is situated below, and in the middle is the breast bone with the semicircular membrane and internal drum membrane.

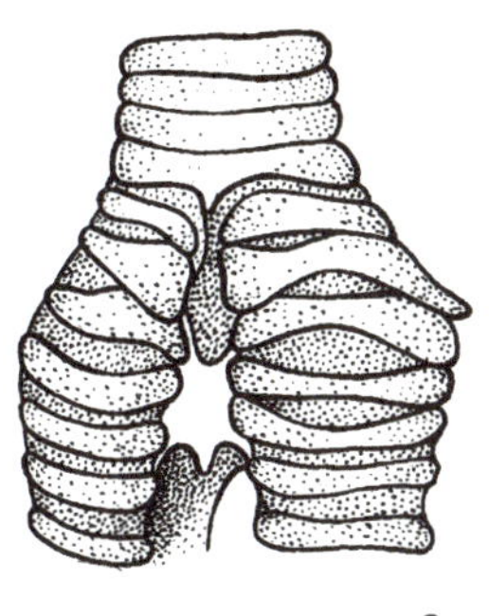

3

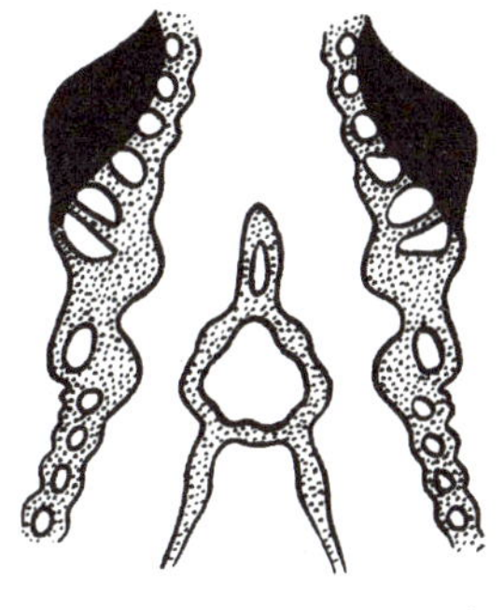

4

The Shama is native to India, Indochina, the Moluccas, Java and Borneo, where it frequents dense woodland and primary forest. In the wild, these birds are relatively cautious.

1 ♂

Spreo Starling (Superb Spreo) *Spreo superbus*

Sturnidae

The Spreo Starling, a glossy, sparkling bird, is kept in a large cage or preferably in an aviary. With a good diet, it can live up to 15 to 20 years, and some specimens have even survived in captivity for 30 years.

This species is fed the Thrush mixture, supplemented daily with a few mealworm larvae or other insects, and fruit. Rowanberries and elderberries should be stored for the winter. Raisins, sunflower, crushed peanuts and hemp seed are also supplied during the winter months. Diluted fruit juice or water sweetened with honey are given to the birds to drink. Spreo Starlings are fond of bathing and should be given large vessels containing water, which are replaced several times a day. In winter, they are housed in heated quarters, at a temperature of 15 to 20 degrees Centigrade. A single bird is easy to tame and pecks up food from the owner's hand.

Spreo Starlings thrive best in a spacious outdoor aviary. They do not hide among the branches but fly around in the front part of the aviary. For breeding purposes, they are given a hollow tree trunk or a wooden nestbox 20 centimetres square and 35 centimetres high. The birds fill it with various materials and line the nest with feathers. The clutch of two to four eggs is incubated by the female for 13 to 15 days. The young stay in the nest for some 3 weeks, and when they are fledged, the parents bring them food for another 14 days. They consume a large quantity of insects.

2

This species is up to 21 centimetres long. The sexes are alike in appearance (1). The beauty of the Spreo Starling is best displayed in the sunshine, when the glossy plumage glitters.

The Spreo Starling is indigenous to eastern Africa. It occurs in Ethiopia, Somalia, Kenya and Tanzania, frequenting forests, lake regions and rivers. It is very fond of water, bathes frequently and often wets all its feathers. It nests in hollow trees (2), often in small colonies. The nesting cup is lined with grass and other plant material. It is aggressive towards other songbirds. After the fledging of the young, Spreo Starlings gather in flocks.

Hill Mynah
Gracula religiosa

Sturnidae

Mynahs are the best imitators of human speech, after parrots, but their talent for 'speaking' varies with the individual and depends on the bird's age. A bird reared by humans is best for this purpose. A talented individual can imitate the pitch of a voice, learn to whistle tunes and repeat the sounds it hears. A newly imported bird soon becomes tame, provided it is in daily contact with its owner and it is allowed to fly about. A well-fed Hill Mynah has beautiful plumage with a metallic gloss and a life expectancy of more than 20 years.

It is fed the Thrush mixture, supplemented with chickweed or other green food. Some large insects, such as crickets, grasshoppers and mealworm larvae, are occasionally served. Fruit and sponge soaked in milk are a regular part ot the diet as well. Mynahs need sunlight and daily bathing. In winter, they are kept in slightly heated quarters. The cage for a single bird must measure at least 100 by 60 by 60 centimetres. The bottom is covered with a sheet of newspaper or peat, which has to be replaced daily, because the excrements are very thin. During the summer, a pair of Hill Mynahs can be housed in an outdoor aviary. They build a nest in a natural hollow or a wooden nestbox, using various materials. The female lays two to three eggs and incubates them for 12 to 14 days.

5

The Hill Mynah occurs in eight subspecies in the Indomalayan region. The subspecies differ in size and in the number of yellow lobes on the head. The nominative subspecies *G. r. religiosa* (1) lives in Borneo; *G. r. indica* (2) inhabits Sri Lanka; *G. r. peninsularis* (3) is found in India; and *G. r. intermedia* (4) lives in Indochina and the Malay Peninsula. Other subspecies are found in the Philippines, Sumatra and Java, the Andaman Islands and Sri Lanka. Their length varies from 24 to 30 centimetres.

In the wild, mynahs frequent mainly treetops, eating fruit and insects. They nest in tree cavities from February to May. The eggs (5) are pale green, speckled, and measure 26 by 36 millimetres. The plumage of the young lacks the gloss and the leathery lobes are *greyish white.*

1

CHARACTERISTICS OF BIRD GROUPS

Valuable background information on species can be obtained from a study of the characteristics, biology and ethology of their order. The following is a brief survey of the orders and families of birds described in this book. The various parts of a bird's body, referred to throughout the text, are shown in Fig. 5.

Order: Galliformes (Game birds)

The species in the order Galliformes described in this book are the King Quail, Californian Quail, Indian Peacock and pheasants, all belonging to the pheasant family (Phasianidae). The common features of all the birds of this order are a short strong beak and powerful digging feet. The Turkey (*Meleagris gallopavo*) and the Capercaillie (*Tetrao urogallus*) are the largest game birds, and the King Quail (*Coturnix chinensis*) is the smallest. As a rule, game birds have skilfully concealed nests on the ground, and lay large clutches. The newly hatched young are covered with down and they can see and walk immediately. All game birds are nidifugous, which means that their offspring can forage for their own food as soon as they hatch, and the hen only guides them to sources of food. Distinct sexual dimorphism, that is, a difference in appearance between the male and the female, exists in most game birds. The cocks usually have more colourful and richer plumage, and they have spurs on their tarsi.

Game birds are predominantly terrestrial, moving speedily and nimbly on the ground. They are reluctant fliers but include some migratory species such as the European Common Quail (*Coturnix coturnix*). At night, some species roost in trees or other elevated places. Game birds have the smallest cerebrum of all birds and their mental abilities are low. They never bathe in water and get rid of dirt by wallowing in dust. Young birds consume chiefly animal food, while adults take seeds and berries.

Some 260 species of the order Galliformes are classified. Aviculturists concentrate mainly on pheasants, in which the males rank among the most colourful birds. Some hens do not sit on their eggs, which have to be transferred to electric incubators, and the hatched chicks are put into an artificial hen (Fig. 6). The source of heat is a bulb or, preferably, a non-luminous radiator. During the first 10 days, the temperature is kept at approximately 35 degrees Centigrade underneath the source. At the age of 2 to 3 weeks, the chicks only sleep under the source, and they gradually stop needing it at all.

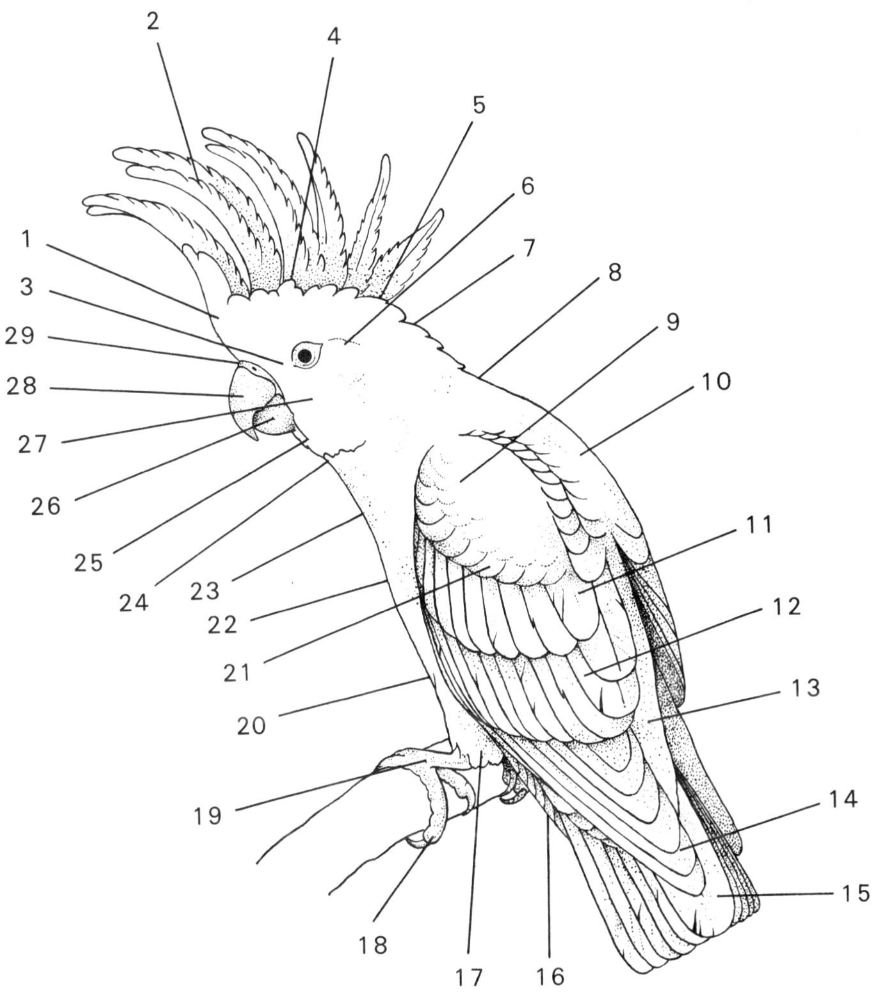

Fig. 5. Topography of a bird's body: 1 — forehead, 2 — crest, 3 — moustaches, 4 — crown, 5 — occipital region, 6 — ear, 7 — nape, 8 — neck, 9 — shoulder, 10 — back, 11 — scapulars, 12 — secondaries, 13 — rump, 14 — primaries, 15 — upper tail coverts, 16 — under tail coverts, 17 — pantalets (tibia) fibula, 18 — toes, 19 — tarsus, 20 — abdomen, 21 — wing coverts, 22 — breast, 23 — crop, 24 — throat, 25 — chin, 26 — lower mandible, 27 — cheek, 28 — upper mandible, 29 — cere

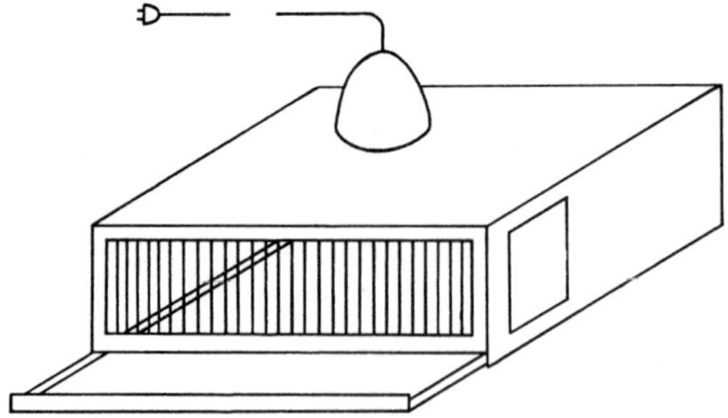

Fig. 6. Artificial sitting hen

Order: Columbiformes (Pigeons and doves)

Columbiformes consist of three families. The sandgrouse family (Pterochididae) comprises only 16 species. The family Raphidae is extinct; its members were exterminated by humans in prehistoric times. Pigeons and doves (Columbidae) represent the most important, numerous and best-known family.

Pigeons and doves are usually medium-sized birds, lacking down. They have a small beak, soft at the base, slightly curved, with nostrils situated in the soft cere. The head is small, and the body is short but stout, particularly in the breast region. The toes are long and short-clawed. Sexual dimorphism does not usually occur. These birds are capable of sustained flight.

Pigeons and doves build rather flimsy nests of twigs in trees, sometimes in cavities, rarely on the ground. The courting males perform nuptial dances, sometimes even nuptial flights, in front of the females. The female usually lays two eggs, two to four times a year. Pigeons and doves are nidicolous birds, that is, the hatched young are helpless. The chicks hatch out blind, covered with down, and parents feed them on a curd-like secretion from the crop. Most pigeons and doves nest in small colonies and move around in flocks. Their diet is almost exclusively vegetarian, composed of seeds and fruits.

Small pigeon or dove species can be kept in the company of small songbirds, while larger ones can be housed with parrots or pheasants. The species which have difficulties with nesting are reared by their readily breeding relatives, such as the Diamond Dove and the Turtle Dove. Pigeons and doves are great favourites with aviculturists because they are hardy and undemanding, breed commonly in captivity and display interesting behaviour.

Order: Trochiliformes (Hummingbirds)

This order consists of the sole but large family of hummingbirds (Trochilidae). Hummingbirds differ from other birds in their wing structure: the scapular bone is the shortest one, the secondary bone is longer and the primary bone is the longest one in the wing. They are well-known for their diminutive size. The smallest species, *Chaetocercus bombus* and *Mellisuga helenae,* weigh approximately 1.9 gram, and the largest species, *Patagona gigas,* attains the size of a Swallow.

The plumage of hummingbirds is splendid, glossy and changeable in colour. The coloration is produced by interference, not by pigmentation. The feathers contain only black pigment, but there is also a layer of specially arranged, colourless, prismatic cells which refract and reflect light. As the bird moves, these cells change position, producing a colourful visual effect on the plumage.

The flight of hummingbirds is also remarkable. Each wing describes a horizontal number eight with such speed that the human eye cannot register the movement. While poised in the air, sucking nectar from blossoms, they flap their wings 54 times per second. In flight, they flap the wings 75 times per second at a speed of 80 kilometres per hour, while during a nuptial or headlong flight, the frequency rises to 200 per second. This requires an enormous energy output and to compensate hummingbirds consume more energy per unit mass than any other animal. Most hummingbirds consume daily three times their body weight in food. The heart represents up to 22 per cent of the total weight and beats 615 times per minute. At night, hummingbirds probably assume a state of torpidity in which their body temperature and metabolism are decreased, allowing them to survive the night chill and fasting. They feed on nectar from flowers and tiny insects. Each species is dependent on specific blossoms, and the beak is adapted to these blossoms, being short or long, curved upwards or downwards, and so on. The tongue has the same function as the proboscis in butterflies: it is long, tubular and can be pushed far out. These birds have short, weak feet and cannot move on the ground.

The nest is built of fine plant material and the outside is covered by moss or lichen. It is cup-shaped and varies in size from a walnut to a coconut. The female lays one to two white eggs which are extremely large in comparison with the bird's body.

In recent years, hummingbirds have been kept more frequently in Europe due to speedy air travel and new methods of transport. The high mortality caused by birds being transported freely in boxes is avoided nowadays by packing each specimen in a kind of flannel jacket (Fig. 7). The transport box is divided into a series of mini-com-

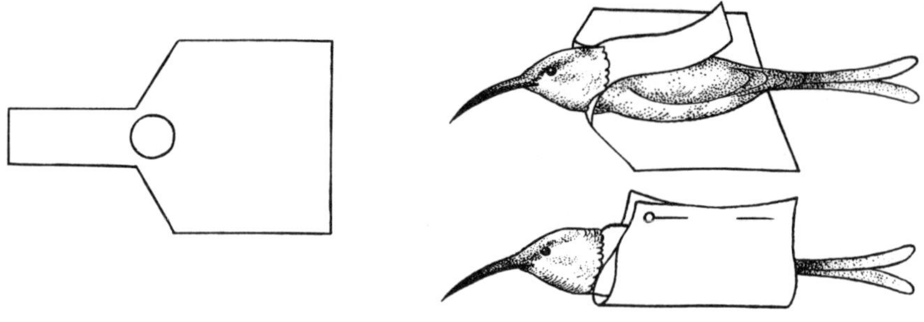

Fig. 7. Wrapping of hummingbirds before transport

partments measuring 2.5 by 2.5 by 10 centimetres, in which the birds are placed with their heads slightly raised. They are fed as often as possible from a syringe fitted with a glass tube, 5 millimetres in diameter. They take the food readily and survive the journey without problems.

Order: Piciformes (Woodpeckers and allies)

The feet of all members of this order are equipped with two toes pointing forward and two pointing backward. Woodpeckers nest in tree cavities or burrows, and their eggs are white and usually spherical. The young are naked and even the adult birds lack down.

Of greatest importance in aviculture is the toucan family (Ramphastidae) comprising 60 species. Toucans have a distinctive beak with an attractive coloration. The colour of the beak varies within each species and probably changes with age and season. In the courtship season, the beak is an important signalling device and may serve as an amplifier. The saw-like edges of the beak help the bird to hold the soft fruit on which it feeds. The tongue is long and narrow, with fibrous, forward-pointing papillae. These are protective scales on the upper and underside of the tarsus, while the sides are unprotected. The young have callous outgrowths on their heels.

In the nesting season, toucans live in pairs. The nesting cavity is situated in trees, often up to 30 metres above the ground, and the nest is unlined. Young birds leave the nest before being fully feathered.

In the wild, toucans live on various soft and pulpous fruits, insects and small vertebrates. In captivity, they become very friendly and are as easy to tame as parrots. They are long-lived if they are well cared for, and may live for several decades.

Order: Psittaciformes (Parrots)

Some 333 species of parrots inhabit tropical and subtropical regions of the Old and New World. Most species live in South America, the Orient and Australia, while some are found in southern Asia and Africa.

The major anatomical feature of parrots is a relatively large skull with a massive and powerful bill which resembles a raptor's bill (Fig. 8). The upper mandible is curved, its tip projects over the lower one, and it can be raised due to a flexible connection with the skull. The rear, rounded edge fits into the ridges in the frontal bones. The inside of the upper mandible is equipped with horny notches which crush food and file the cutting edges of the lower mandible. The soft and muscular tongue is a sensitive tactile organ used to hold food or lick it. In some species, the tongue is enveloped by a horny layer, while in others it is covered by tuft-like taste buds. The tarsus is short and strong, covered by small horny scales. Two toes (second and third) point forward and two others (first and fourth) point backward. This arrangement allows dexterous climbing and the holding or passing of food. The preening gland in the rump is stunted or completely absent, and parrots consequently do not grease their plumage but powder it instead. The well-developed down breaks down continuously into a large quantity of dust particles which prevent water from penetrating to the skin.

Some parrots are fast and skilful fliers, while others fly clumsily. They are sociable birds, which nest in pairs and gather in large flocks outside the nesting season. Most species do not migrate.

The male and female usually form a pair for life. Parrots nest predominantly in tree cavities, sometimes in burrows, and exceptionally

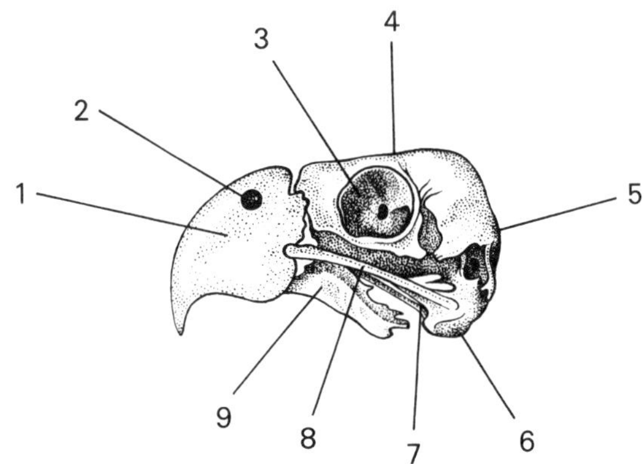

Fig. 8. Topography of a parrot's skull: 1 — upper mandible/maxilla, 2 — nasal cavity, 3 — eye cavity, 4 — frontal bone/os frontale, 5 — pariental bone/os parientale, 6 — occipital bone/os occipitale, 7 — quadrate bone/os quadratum, 8 — quadrate-jugal bone/os quadrato-jugale, 9 — articular bone/os articulare

in termite mounds. Only one species, the Monk Parakeet, builds a nest. Large species rear one brood a year and the clutch contains two eggs as a rule. Small species breed two to three times a year and each clutch numbers six to eight eggs.

The diet is composed of various seeds, flower buds, fruits of trees and bushes, tubers, and even insects and their larvae. Parrots have the best-developed brain of all birds and they are capable of non-notional thinking. They can remember a few dozen words including whole sentences, and they learn to associate them with specific situations, although they are not able to understand their meaning. Owing to their beauty and intelligence, parrots are the most popular birds with aviculturists.

Order: Passeriformes (Songbirds)

Songbirds form the largest bird order, surpassing in numbers all the other bird species put together. This book introduces species of various families: babbling thrushes (Timaliidae), tanagers (Thraupidae), sugar birds (Coerebidae), finches (Fringillidae), weavers (Ploceidae), waxbills (Estrildidae), thrushes (Turdidae) and starlings (Sturnidae). All songbirds have a similar anatomical structure characterized by special cranial bones, an identical number of cervical vertebrae and four toes on the hind limb. Three toes point forward (second, third and fourth), one points backward (first). The preening gland is always present and covered with feathers. The vermiform appendix is stunted. Only a few species have down feathers. The weight ranges from 4 grams to 1.7 kilograms.

Songbirds are usually accomplished fliers and many migrate in autumn to regions which have a more favourable climate and food supply during the winter months. The nest is built on the ground, in bushes, trees, cavities, burrows or on rocks. The eggs are either plain or spotted. Incubation takes 11 to 21 days, except in the Australian Lyrebird (*Menura novaehollandiae*) which sits on the clutch for 42 days. The young when they hatch are blind and bare (again except the Lyrebird). All songbirds are nidicolous and they feed their young by putting the food into their gapes. They have keen eyesight, which helps them to obtain their food. Many songbirds are exclusively insectivorous, while others are vegetarian or live on a mixed diet. Most species are good songsters with similarly shaped vocal organs.

Songbirds are great favourites with aviculturists because of their gay coloration, simple feeding and easy breeding. Species of the families Estrildidae, Fringillidae, Turdidae and Sturnidae are the most frequently kept songbirds.

HYGIENE AND VETERINARY PROBLEMS IN BIRD-KEEPING

Any bird can fall ill despite good care. It must be treated and unless the disease can be identified by the aviculturist, the bird has to be taken to a veterinary surgeon specializing in birds. Prevention, however, is the main task of every aviculturist. This begins with quarantine of newly acquired birds, hygiene and disinfection of cages and aviaries, and early diagnosis and separation of any affected bird. The cage or aviary must be kept clean and all remnants of food and excrements removed regularly. The housing and all the objects within it are mechanically cleaned and washed down with commonly used disinfectants, following the instructions concerning the concentration, repetition and duration of effects. Many germs are destroyed by freezing weather. Food containers which are not ruined by high temperatures can be disinfected by submerging them in boiling water for 30 to 60 minutes. Concrete water pools and other objects in the aviary can be scorched by flame for 30 seconds.

An inexperienced bird-keeper may not realize that a bird is unwell.

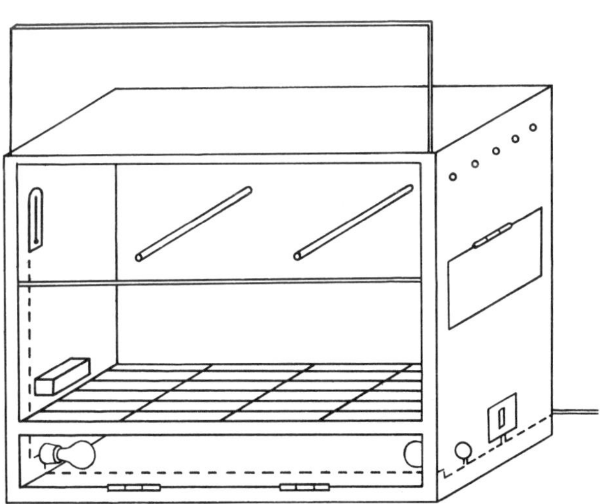

Fig. 9. Hospital cage: 1 — sliding glass wall, 2 — air holes, 3 — light bulbs, 4 — light switch, 5 — asbestos bottom, 6 — thermometer.

A sick bird ruffles its feathers, its eyes are dull, it is silent and sleeps much of the time, it does not preen its plumage, and it perches near the feeding vessel without eating. Such a bird should be isolated from the others and transferred to a hospital cage. It is extremely important to do this as early as possible. The hospital cage (Fig. 9) is a box with the front wall made of glass and with air holes in the upper part. Its size should allow the bird to turn around. Two to three low-wattage light bulbs are situated underneath the asbestos bottom (this arrangement permits easier regulation than a single strong source of heat) to heat the cage at 35 to 40 degrees Centigrade. A moist filter paper or a wet cloth are hung in the cage, or a tray with water is put near one of the bulbs, to ensure sufficient humidity.

Although a sick bird may not take any food or only a small quantity, food has to be available all the time. It must be easy to digest, so green food and egg mixture are best omitted. Weak camomile tea or ordinary tea are served instead of water. Isolating the bird in the hospital cage and regulating the heating provides better conditions for observation and diagnosis. Parasitologic and bacteriologic analyses of excrements, may be necessary for diagnosis. Excrements should be examined for preventive purposes once every six months. If the owner is not certain how to proceed with treatment, a veterinary surgeon specializing in bird diseases should be consulted immediately. As soon as the diagnosis is made, treatment can begin.

This book cannot list all the bird diseases and their treatment, but the following is a survey of major ones.

Parasitic diseases

These are a frequent cause of death among captive birds. As long as a balance is maintained between the host and the parasite, the symptoms are difficult to recognize. The sick bird sits listlessly and hardly moves.

Endoparasites invade body organs. The presence of their eggs can be ascertained by microscopic examination of the bird's excreta. They include various ascarids (*Ascaris*), worms of the genus *Capillaria* and roundworms (*Heterakis*). Ascarids and *Capillaria* live in the small intestine, and the latter can also be found in the oesophagus and crop. The dosage of medicine depends on the size of the bird and should be decided by a veterinary surgeon. When the worms are eliminated, the cage or aviary should be thoroughly disinfected to destroy any remaining eggs. Perches and branches should be replaced by new ones. The treatment is in some cases repeated after 3 weeks unless the veterinary surgeon advises against it. Some 6 weeks from the beginning of the treatment the excreta of the affected birds are re-examined for eggs.

Syngamosis is caused by the parasitic worm *Syngamus trachea* which lives attached to the mucous membrane of the trachea and feeds on blood. The symptoms of this disease are not very conspicuous; the bird opens the beak, yawns, breathes with difficulty and coughs. Reliable diagnosis can be made only by the microscopic examination of the excreta. The bird coughs up the eggs of *Syngamus trachea* into the gape, swallows them and subsequently excretes them. The eggs hatch into larvae in the ground and penetrate the bodies of temporary hosts, such as earthworms and snails. A bird may then peck up a larva or infected earthworm, and catch the disease. Treatment should be carried out by a vet.

Ectoparasites live on the skin and plumage, or inside the skin. The birds become restless, anaemic, lose weight, and, if affected by great numbers of these parasites, they die. The most common ectoparasites are mites (*Acarina*) and bird lice (*Mallophaga*). The tiny mite *Dermanyssus,* about 0.6 millimetres long, sucks the birds' blood at night and hides by day in crevices inside the cage. If the cage is covered overnight with a large white sheet, the mites can be visible in the morning as miniature red dots. *Dermanyssus* can become a carrier of some infectious diseases. All the equipment in the cage, the bottom and walls, and the birds themselves should be dusted with an insecticide, and the treatment repeated several times. The legs, beak and cloacal area may be affected by the mite *Chemidocoptes* which causes sponge-like and scab-like outgrowths known as scabies of the leg. Olive oil can be applied to the affected spot. Treatment is continued until the symptoms disappear. Bird lice (*Mallophaga*) feed on feathers and scales of the skin. They live on their host and make the birds restless and irritated. When the bird is heavily affected, the eggs can be seen on the tips of small feathers. Strips of special insecticides can be hung in the room for about 4 months. They must not come into contact with the birds or their food.

Contagious diseases

Salmonellosis (paratyphoid) is caused by the *Salmonella* bacteria. The main symptoms are acute diarrhoea and generally bad condition. The bird is listless, sleepy, weak, refuses food, suffers from thirst, shivers, and so on. There are many types of salmonellosis and their courses differ. The disease always affects all the birds kept together, and can be transmitted to humans and other animals. The main carriers of infection are mice and infected wild birds such as sparrows.

The disease can be identified by microscopic analysis of the excreta. Treatment must be undertaken by a veterinary specialist.

Ornithosis and psittacosis are diseases caused by microorganisms which form a stage between viruses and rickettsia. Psittacosis, also called 'parrot fever', is more dangerous than ornithosis, and it has fortunately become rare. Both diseases may be transmitted to humans. The symptoms of psittacosis are clogged nasal cavities, coughing, difficulty in breathing, diarrhoea, lethargy, sleepiness, weakness and thirst. In adult birds, ornithosis usually evidences no outward symptoms, but the young suffer from respiratory problems and disorders of the digestive tract. The incubation period for both diseases is 3 to 30 days, sometimes longer. A veterinary specialist must always be consulted. These diseases can be successfully treated.

Epithelioma and diphtheria are two forms of a disease caused by the virus *Borreliota fringillae,* affecting predominantly game birds, pigeons and doves, and finch-type songbirds. Epithelioma appears mainly on the unfeathered parts of the body, for example, the eyelids and the area around the beak. It appears as nodules under the skin which change from pale to dark and finally turn into scabs. Diphtheria usually begins by a head cold. The mucous membranes of the mouth and oesophagus become covered with a yellowish coating which later firmly adheres to the membranes and, if it is torn off, the membranes bleed slightly. Accompanying symptoms are conjunctivitis and inflammation of the cornea.

Diseases of the digestive tract

These are the most common health problems in birds. They are chiefly the result of incorrect feeding, particularly the serving of spoiled or contaminated food, harmful additives and sudden dietary changes. Inflammation of the crop manifests itself as a marked enlargement of this organ which becomes soft and pliable. A sick bird frequently vomits the mucous, mushy contents of the crop or whole undigested seeds. The crop has to be emptied by massages repeated every other day. The bird is given easily digestible food and camomile tea. A blocked (tough) crop is stuffed with undigested and indigestible material, and is enlarged and hard. Again if this is suspected you should consult your vet. Inflammation of the intestines and stomach is revealed by diarrhoea and overall symptoms such as lethargy, sleepiness, ruffled plumage and lack of appetite. Green food and fruit must be dropped immediately from the diet and camomile tea served instead of water. The bird should be transferred to a hospital cage and the ambient temperature increased to approximately 30 degrees Centigrade. Sick insectivorous birds are given a minimum of their staple food. Antibiotics are administered if the condition does not improve, but a specialist should always be consulted.

Respiratory diseases

Even an experienced bird-keeper may find these diseases difficult to identify. The symptoms can be a weak yellowish discharge from the nasal openings and breathing difficulties, such as snorting and sneezing. In more severe cases the bird displays general symptoms. Treatment of respiratory diseases is possible only in mild cases and at the onset of the disease. The bird is placed in a separate cage at a steady and humid temperature of 30 degrees Centigrade. If the disease is provoked by infection, antibiotics prescribed by a veterinary surgeon have to be administered.

Eye inflammations

These are caused by injuries or infection, the latter being more common in newly imported birds. The sick bird has reddish running eyes, a suppurating discharge and its eyelids are stuck by pus. Bathing of the eyes in boric acid is sufficient in mild cases. However, a severe inflammation requires treatment by eye drops prescribed by a veterinary surgeon.

Disorders of the metabolism

A major disorder of the metabolism affecting birds is gout. It is caused by an unbalanced diet (excess of protein) and accumulation of uric acid in the kidneys and in the joints, which become swollen, painfull and tough. The curative diet is free of protein and rich in green food.

Feather plucking may make the bird unsightly and is a health disorder. The causes can range from lack of certain nutrients, wrong diet, boredom and a dry environment, to exaggerated sexual instinct. Improvement is sometimes very difficult. The diet should be checked to ensure the correct supply of vitamins, minerals and proteins, and in some birds even 'occupational therapy', can help. Vitamin deficiency (avitaminosis) is a result of an unbalanced diet. There are many types of avitaminosis and many vitamin preparations which can be served to repair the deficiency. The best cure is a diet rich in natural foods containing vitamins.

Egg binding

The females of some species, particularly young ones, may experience difficulty in expulsion of the egg in sudden cold weather. The female ruffles her feathers and sleeps most of the time. The egg can be felt in the cloaca. The female should be placed in a warm, humid environment, oil is carefully applied into the cloaca, and the belly is gently massaged towards the cloacal opening.

Overgrown claws and beaks

Older birds often suffer from these. Thicker perches with rougher surfaces help the birds to wear their claws and beaks naturally. They can also be given lime or grit stones purchased in special shops to file their beaks on. If necessary, the beak and claws should be clipped with sharp nail clippers or scissors and trimmed with a nail file.

Index

Agaporis cana 82
fischeri 86
personata 88
roseicollis 84
Alisterus scapularis 54
Amadina erythrocephala 166
fasciata 168
Amandava amandava 172
subflava 170
Amazon, Blue-fronted 124
Tucuman 120
Yellow-shouldered 122
Amazona aestiva 124
barbadensis 122
tucumana 120
Ara ambigua 98
ararauna 96
chloroptera 102
macao 100
militaris 98
severa 104
Aratinga aurea 112
cactorum 110
jendaya 108
wagleri 106

Bathilda ruficauda 184
Budgerigar 76
Bunting, Indigo 142
Nonpareil 140

Cacatua alba 48
galerita 44
sulphurea 42
moluccensis 46
Cacatuidae 42–51
Calospiza fastuosa 132
Calypte anna 127
Canary 144
Cardinal, Red-crested 136
Virginian 138
Calospiza fastuosa 132
Chrysolophus amherstiae 24
pictus 22
Cockatiel 50
Cockatoo, Greater White-crested 48
Lesser Sulphur-crested 42
Salmon-crested 46
Sulphur-crested 44
Coerebidae 134
Colibri coruscans 127
serrirostris 127
Columbidae 30–36
Columbiformes 210
Combassou 154
Conure, Cactus 110
Nanday 114
Peach-fronted 112
Red-fronted 106
Yendaya 108
Copsychus malabaricus 202
Cordon Bleu 162
Coryphospingus cristatus 146
Coturnix chinensis 16
Cyanerpes cyaneus 134
Cyanoramphus auriceps 68

Dove, Cape 36
Diamond 32

Eclectus roratus 52
Emblema guttata 180
Erythrura gouldiae 178
psittacea 176
trichroa 174
Estrilda melpoda 156
troglodytes 158
Estrildidae 156–201
Euodice contans 200
malabarica 201
Euplectes franciscana 148

Finch, Amaduvade 172
Bengalese 198
Black-ringed 186
Black-throated 190
Blue-faced 174
Crimson 182
Cut-throat 168
Double-barred 186
Gouldian 178
Parrot 176
Red-crested 146
Red-headed 166
Ribbon 168
Spice 196
Star 184
Zebra 188
Fire-finch, Common 160
Firetail, Diamond 180

Fringillidae 136—47
Forpus coelestis 119
cyanopygius 119
passerinus 118
xanthops 119
xanthopterygius 119

Gallicolumba luzonica 34
Galliformes 208
Gennaeus nycthemerus 26
Geopelia cuneata 32
Gracula religiosa 206

Hypochera chalybeata 154
Hummingbird 126, 211, 212

Lagonostica senegala 160
Leiothrix lutea 130
Lonchura malacca 194
punctulata 196
Lophornis adorabilis 127
Lophortyx californica 18
Loriidae 38—41
Lorikeet, Rainbow 38
Lorius lory 40
Lory, Blue-tailed 40
Lovebird, Fischer's 86
Grey-headed 82
Masked 88
Peach-faced 84

Macaw, Blue and Yellow 96
Chestnut-fronted 104
Green-winged 102
Military 98
Red and Yellow 100
Scarlet 100
Mannikin, Nutmeg 196
Three-coloured 194
Melopsittacus undulatus 76
Myiopsitta monachus 116
Mynah, Hill 206

Nandayus nenday 114
Neochmia phaeton 182
Neophema bourkii 70
pulchella 72
splendida 74

Ocyphaps lophotes 30
Oena capensis 36

Padda oryzivora 192
Parakeet, Alexandrine 90
Monk 116
Plum-headed 94
Rose-ringed 92
Paroaria coronata 136
Parrot, Bourke's 70
Eclectus 52
Grey 78
King 54
Princess 56
Red-rumped 66
Scarlet-breasted 74
Senegal 80
Turquoise 72
Yellow-fronted 68
Parrotlet, Green-rumped 118
Passeriformes 214
Passerina ciris 140
cyanea 142
Pavo cristatus 28
Peafowl, Indian 28
Phasianidae 16—29
Pheasant, Golden 22
Lady Amherst's 24
Reeve's 20
Silver 26
Piciformes 212
Pigeon, Bleeding-heart 34
Crested 30
Platycercus adscitus 62
elegans 58
eximius 60
icterotis 64
Ploceidae 148—55
Poephila acuticauda 190
Poicephalus senegalus 80
Polytelis alexandrae 56
Psephotus haematonotus 66
Psittacidae 52—125
Psittaciformes 213
Psittacula cyanocephala 94
eupatria 90
krameri 92
Psittacus erithacus 78
Pyrrhuloxia cardinalis 138

Quail, Californian 18
King 16
Quelea quelea 150

Ramphastidae 128

Ramphastos cuvieri 129
sulphurata 129
toco 129
Rice-bird 192
Robin, Pekin 130
Rosella, Crimson 58
Eastern 60
Pale-headed 62
Western 64

Sappho sparganura 127
Serinus canaria 144
Shama 202
Silverbill, African 200
Indian 201
Sparrow, Java 192
Paradise 166
Spreo, Superb 204
Spreo superbus 204
Starling, Spreo 204
Steganura paradisea 152
Stizoptera bichenowii 186
Sturnidae 204—207
Sugar Bird, Yellow-winged 134
Syrmaticus reevesii 20

Taeniopygia guttata 188
Tanager, Superb 132
Thraupidae 132
Timaliidae 130
Topaza bella 127
Toucan 128
Trichoglossus haematodus 38
Trochilidae 126
Trochiliformes 211
Turdidae 202

Uraeginthus bengalus 162
granatinus 164

Waxbill, Golden-breasted 170
Orange-cheeked 156
Red-eared 158
Violet-eared 164
Weaver, Orange 148
Red-billed 150
Whydah, Paradise 152